For Faith and Freedom

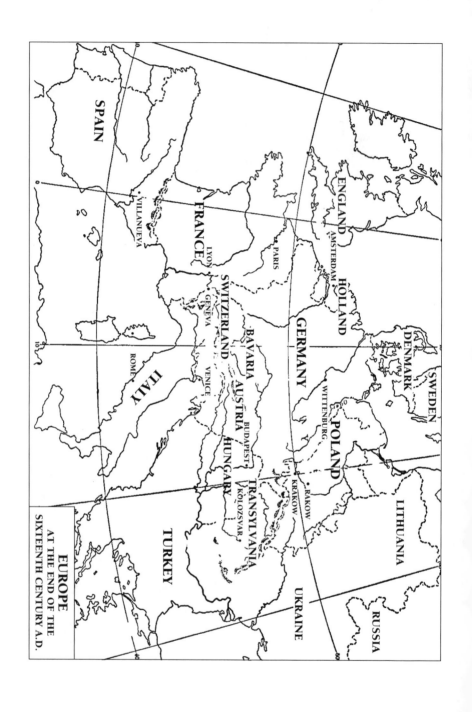

EUROPE
AT THE END OF THE
SIXTEENTH CENTURY A.D.

SPAIN

FRANCE

ENGLAND

HOLLAND

AMSTERDAM

GERMANY

DENMARK

SWEDEN

POLAND

LITHUANIA

RUSSIA

VILLANUEVA

LYON

PARIS

SWITZERLAND

GENEVA

BAVARIA

ITALY

ROME

VENICE

AUSTRIA

HUNGARY

BUDAPEST

WITTENBURG

KRAKOW

RAKOW

UKRAINE

TRANSYLVANIA

KOLOZSVAR

TURKEY

For Faith and Freedom

A Short History of Unitarianism in Europe

Charles A. Howe

Skinner House Books
Boston

Published by Skinner House Books, an imprint of the Unitarian Universalist Association of Congregations, 25 Beacon Street, Boston, MA 02108-2800.

Printed in the USA.

ISBN 1-55896-359-6
978-1-55896-359-7

10 9 8 7 6 5 4
12 11 10 09

Acknowledgments
The map of sixteenth-century Europe is adapted from *Our Unitarian Heritage* by Earl Morse Wilber. Copyright © 1925 by Beacon Press, renewed 1953 by Earl Morse Wilber. Used by permission of Beacon Press, Boston.
    The portrait of Michael Servetus is from *Hunted Heretic* by Roland H. Bainton. Copyright © 1953 by Beacon Press. Used by permission of Beacon Press, Boston.
    The portrait of Francis Dávid at the Diet of Torda is by Körösföi Kriesch Aladár. The original hangs in the Museum of Torda, Romania. This copy is from the library of Dr. Judit Gellérd, Center for Free Religion, Chico, California.
    The portrait of Theophilus Lindsey is provided by the UUA archives.
    The photo of the International Council of Unitarians and Universalists is from the library of Polly Guild.

To John C. Godbey
mentor, colleague, and friend

Contents

Foreword

I first had the pleasure of meeting Charles Howe in 1978 when I was a student at Manchester College, Oxford, and he was a visiting scholar on study leave doing research on Universalism in Great Britain. He impressed me then as a man of learning, sensitivity, and personal charm, eager to learn about the faith of others as a way of strengthening his own faith. His previous publications have confirmed the justice of his reputation as one of our most valued contemporary historians.

Charles Howe's great gift is to make history accessible. In his lively and engaging writing style, he offers the readers of *For Faith and Freedom* a judicious overview of all the important trends and milestones in the history of Unitarianism in Europe. In so doing, he has made an important contribution toward all Unitarian Universalists' understanding and appreciation of their faith, and he has provided some valuable guideposts for the future.

At a time in our world history when connections between existing Unitarians and Universalists around the world are being strengthened, and churches and fellowships are being established in countries where there has never before been a Unitarian Universalist presence, Charles Howe has made an important scholarly contribution.

I am pleased to commend his work to anyone with an interest in the future of Unitarian Universalism, as well as in its history.

The Reverend Dr. David Usher
President, International Council of
Unitarians and Universalists

Preface

In 1952 the second volume of Earl Morse Wilbur's *A History of Unitarianism* was published, marking the completion of the first comprehensive study of the Unitarian movement. This volume, an account of Unitarianism in Transylvania, England, and America, had been preceded seven years earlier by one covering Polish Socinianism and its antecedents. A half century later Wilbur's two volumes remain the basic work in this field, of fundamental importance to scholars, especially since many of the primary sources were destroyed during the Second World War. As a result of his study Wilbur identified a common thread connecting the more or less independent components of the movement, one based less on theology than on the basic principles of freedom, reason, and tolerance. Ever since, those defining Unitarianism have regularly cited these three principles.

The research behind this history occupied Wilbur for over forty years, and the writing was his chief work for fifteen. A fascinating account of why and how the work was undertaken is given in the *Proceedings of the Unitarian Historical Society*, Volume IX, Part I (1951). At the time the two volumes were published, Wilbur was emeritus president and professor at the Pacific Unitarian School for the Ministry, since renamed the Starr King School for the Ministry, an institution that he had helped found in 1905 and had served as its first president. The school is committed to the continuing availability and use of his history and has recently dedicated a new reading room in his memory.

In 1962, a decade after Wilbur's second volume appeared, George Huntston Williams of the Harvard Divinity School published his monumental work, *The Radical Reformation*, the third edition of which appeared thirty years later. Williams's work is somewhat longer than Wilbur's (1,513 pages as compared to 1,135) and broader in scope, covering the history of the left wing of the Reformation as a whole, with detailed attention given not only to the Unitarians, but also to the Anabaptists, Evangelicals, and others. Together the two histories provide a detailed study of the emergence of anti-trinitarianism and Unitarianism during the sixteenth century, with Wilbur extending his coverage through the nineteenth and to a limited extent into the early part of the twentieth. This present volume includes as its final chapter a brief overview of twentieth-century Unitarianism in Europe as a whole.

The writing of this short history was originally inspired by my experience in teaching introductory courses in Unitarian Universalist history at leadership schools and summer institutes, to adult education classes in parish settings, and to Unitarian Universalist students at Wesley Theological Seminary in Washington, DC; in all these instances the availability of such a book would have been extremely helpful. I also wrote it to bring the essence of Wilbur's and Williams's work to the general reader—to those without the time and motivation to undertake the formidable task of studying either of these lengthy histories in all their complexity, but who nevertheless wish to gain an understanding of the history of European Unitarianism and its importance to contemporary religious liberalism.

Certainly American Unitarian Universalists are increasingly interested in gaining such an understanding as the network connecting liberal religionists around the world continues to expand. The recently organized International Council of Unitarians and Universalists (ICUU); the current Partner Church Project linking American congregations with those in Romania, Hungary, and Czechoslovakia; and the ongoing work of the International Association for Religious Freedom (IARF) all give evidence of this expansion. Finally, I hope that at least some readers of this short history will be inspired to go on to a serious study of Wilbur's *A History of Unitarianism* and Williams's *The Radical Reformation*.

It is worth noting that the British historian, Jeremy Goring, in his article "Unitarianism: History, Myth, or Make-Believe?" in the *Transactions of the Unitarian Historical Society*, Vol. XIX, No. 4 (April 1990), has criticized Wilbur's treatment of the history of English Unitarianism on a number of counts: the latter's use of the metaphor of a stream (there are too many "unconnected whirlpools" and divisions; a "tree" would be better); his failure to recognize the role of women (Wilbur mentions only four: Queen Mary, Queen Elizabeth, Lady Hewley, and Queen Victoria—none of them Unitarians); his emphasis (Goring would say overemphasis) on Unitarianism as a body of ideas rather than the story of people; and his insufficient recognition of the importance of the original Dissenters (they, rather than John Biddle, qualify as the "fathers" of the movement). Goring's criticisms seem cogent, and I have taken them into account. The American feminist historian, Cynthia Grant Tucker, has also noted Wilbur's masculine bias in her paper "When History Speaks in a Woman's Voice," presented at the Earl Morse Wilbur History Colloquium at Starr King in January 1994 and appearing in its *Proceedings*. Such bias is a trait common to Wilbur's generation and one that by no means has been yet overcome.

This book is almost entirely derivative in contents, with its organizational plan for the most part following that of Wilbur. No treatment of American Unitarianism is included, however, since most readers will already be knowledgeable about this subject or can readily consult other sources. Because this book is written primarily for the general reader and because its contents are chiefly derivative, I have not included references to sources in the body of the text. Readers who wish to identify sources can do so by referring to the section on References.

A number of unfamiliar proper names appear in this book. For the period covered by the two volumes of Wilbur's *A History of Unitarianism*, I have followed for the most part Wilbur's usage in the spelling of proper names. For example, the Latin name Laelius Socinus has been used rather than the Italian name Lelio Sozzini and the partially anglicized name Francis Dávid rather than the Hungarian name Dávid Ferenc. For the period following the Second World War, Hungarian names have been used wherever appropriate, though the order of family and given names has been reversed. Thus the name of the late bishop of the Unitarian Church of Romania is given as János Erdö, rather than Erdö János, the Hungarian form, or John Erdö, the partially anglicized form. Places in Transylvania are usually known by both Hungarian and Romanian names, and sometimes by a German name as well. Following Wilbur's usage, only the Hungarian name has been used; for example, Kolozsvár rather than Kluj-Napoca.

I appreciate the encouragement to write this book that I have received both from the students in the courses I have taught and from numerous colleagues who have reinforced my conviction that it will fill an important unmet need.

My appreciation also goes out to many people for their help, direct or indirect, in its preparation: to the late Mitchell B. Garrett, Professor of European History at the University of North Carolina at Chapel Hill, who first fostered my interest in the Reformation during my undergraduate days; to John Godbey, Professor of Church History at the Meadville/Lombard Theological School, whom I have considered my mentor for the past thirty years and to whom this book is dedicated; to David B. Parke, who first stimulated my interest in Unitarian Universalist history prior to my going into the ministry; to Alan Seaburg, recently retired Curator of Manuscripts at the Andover-Harvard Theological Library, an unfailing source of information, resources, and encouragement; to the late Bishop János Erdö, Mózes Kedei, Dénes Katona, Judit Gellérd, Richard Beal, Rudy Nemser, Judith Wright, George K. Beach, Donald Harrington, Peter Raible, Leon Hopper, and Morris Hudgins for information and criticism on twentieth-century Unitarianism in Romania and Hungary; to Alan Ruston, Andrew Hill, Matthew Smith, David Usher, Kenneth MacLean,

Phillip Hewett, David Wykes, and Richard Boeke for information and criticism on twentieth-century Unitarianism in Great Britain; to Usher, MacLean, and Harrington for information and criticism on twentieth-century European Unitarianism in general; to Nada Velimirovíc for supplying the name of Jadwige Gnoinskiej, benefactress of Raków; to Patricia Frevert and Brenda Wong of Skinner House Books for their ongoing help and cooperation; to my wife Ann for leading me into the computer age; and, of course, to Earl Morse Wilbur, George Huntston Williams, and all the others whose scholarship provided the materials out of which this book has been created.

Charles A. Howe
Raleigh, North Carolina
September 1996

Michael Servetus (1511–1553)

Theophilus Lindsey (1723–1808)

Francis Dávid (1510–1579) at the Diet of Torda, 1568.

The delegates from 16 countries and observers who gathered at Essex, MA, March 1995, for the Founding Meeting of the International Council of Unitarians and Universalists.

"As for the Trinity . . . "

*Now the catholic faith is this: that we worship one God
in a Trinity and the Trinity is a unity; neither con-
founding the persons, nor dividing the substance. For
there is one person of the Father, another of the Son,
another of the Holy Spirit. But the divinity of the
Father, and of the Son, and of the Holy Spirit, is one,
the glory equal, the majesty co-eternal.*

——THE ATHANASIAN CREED

*O*n February 9, 1533, Philip Melanchthon wrote his friend
Joachim Camerarius expressing concern about a book that
had been published two years before, *On the Errors of the
Trinity,* by Michael Servetus. "I find Servetus acute and subtle
enough in disputation, but not very solid. . . . On justification
he is plainly demented. As for the Trinity you know I have
always feared this would break out some day. Good God, what
tragedies this question will excite among those who come
after us!"

Melanchthon had good reason to be worried. Along with
Martin Luther, Ulrich Zwingli, and John Calvin, he was a
leader of the Protestant Reformation then breaking out in the
Roman Catholic Church. Only three years earlier at the Diet of
Augsburg (an assembly of the nobles of the region of Augsburg
in Germany), he had prepared the Protestant statement for
imperial approval, taking pains to point out that the Reformers differed from the Roman church, not on points of doctrine,
but only with respect to practice. One purpose of the statement was to ease some of the tensions between the Protestant
Reformers and the church of the Holy Roman Empire. And

now this upstart Spaniard, Michael Servetus, was attacking the most sacred doctrine of the Roman church in a way that was certain to create a problem for the whole Protestant movement.

In actuality, up until then the doctrine of the Trinity had held far less importance for the Reformers than it did for Rome, and, without denying it, they had tended to discount it as being unscriptural and therefore unessential. Melanchthon himself had said, "There is no reason why we should pay much attention to the profoundest subjects about God, his unity, his trinity. What, pray, have scholastic theologians in all the centuries gained by dealing with these subjects alone? When Paul in his Epistle to the Romans drew up a short statement of Christian doctrine, he did not philosophize on the mysteries of the Trinity, did he?" Luther thought the term "Trinity" had a cold sound to it and omitted it from his catechism and liturgy. Calvin disapproved of the Athanasian Creed and touched but lightly on the doctrine in his catechism. But once Melanchthon's fears had been realized and the question of the Trinity had broken out, the Reformers, fearing a controversy destructive to their cause, quickly gave the doctrine their strong support. A few like Servetus did not, and thus was the Unitarian movement born.

Unitarianism has traditionally been defined theologically as a Christian heresy that denies the doctrine of the Trinity and affirms instead God's unity. Clearly, modern Unitarianism, as embodied in the Unitarian Universalist Association and elsewhere, has moved well beyond this definition and, in fact, such a definition was probably never adequate. As Earl Morse Wilbur stated a half century ago in his *A History of Unitarianism*, the movement's "consistent adherence to the unipersonality of God and the subordinate rank of Christ may almost be said to be incidental to the movement rather than essential to it." And he went on to characterize Unitarianism, not in terms of theology (for there has seldom been agreement on that score—even Wilbur's statement on "consistent adherence" could be disputed), but rather in terms of a growing commitment to three basic principles: complete freedom of religious thought; the unrestricted use of reason; and tolerance of differing views and practices.

It was, however, rejection of the orthodox doctrine of the Trinity that first brought the Unitarian movement into being; hence it is important to understand why and how that doctrine originated, how it became so firmly established, and why there were those who felt compelled to reject it.

Christianity began in the first century CE in Palestine. It was originally a movement within Judaism whose adherents considered Jesus to be the promised Messiah ("Christ" in Greek), a man sent by God, but a man, nevertheless. For them to have attributed divinity to Jesus would have been unthinkable, completely contrary to their Jewish concept of the oneness of God. But as Christianity moved out into the gentile, or non-Jewish, world and became more and more detached from its Jewish roots, this understanding of Jesus was largely lost, being replaced by understandings based on Greek philosophy. As a result, the role of the *Logos*, or "Word" of John's Gospel in the Bible, became of central importance: "In the beginning was the Word, and the Word was with God, and the Word was God. . . . And the Word became flesh and dwelt among us. . . ." A Greek concept dating back to the sixth century BCE, *Logos* referred to a divine principle regulating all things and manifesting itself so that human beings might perceive it. Its use in John's Gospel inevitably led to speculations that Jesus was not only human, but in some sense divine; thus was the down-to-earth Christianity of Jewish origin forced into the abstract structure of Greek philosophy.

During the first few centuries the Christian church, various emerging groups attempted to spell out the relationship between God, *Logos*, and Jesus; all such attempts had their weaknesses. Not only were they extremely abstract, but they tended to suggest the existence of more than one deity, something quite unacceptable to most Christians. At the same time, many Christians felt that these formulations failed to give proper status to Jesus, the Christ, invariably making him inferior to God. As a consequence, a number of Christian sects proposed solutions purporting to affirm both the unity of God and the preeminence of Christ as the Savior of the world.

One such solution, proposed by the Sabellians (named after a Roman Christian named Sabellius), claimed that God existed in three different "modes," but only in one mode at a time. God's different names—Father, Son, and Holy Spirit (for at various points in the scriptures all three are referred to as God)—described the various roles God played at different times. Two other groups, the Docetists and the Gnostics, rejected any notion that Christ was human, asserting that he was not a material being in any sense, but only *appeared* to be human; in fact, the Gnostics went so far as to claim that the entire material world was inherently evil and that only the spiritual was good. (Incidentally, according to scholar Elaine Pagels, the Gnostics were the one Christian sect that gave equal status to women.) Many of the views espoused by these various sects came to be known as heresies by the emerging mainstream of the Christian church.

By the fourth century, Gnosticism had been effectively suppressed in the Roman Empire as heretical and the Jewish Christian sects had by-and-large died out. Nevertheless, a wide variety of opinions still existed as to the nature of both God and Jesus, and no clear consensus was beginning to emerge. By then the growing Christian church had begun to organize itself along hierarchical lines, and when Alexander, the bishop of Alexandria in Egypt, attempted to bring some resolution to the matter, a controversy erupted. Alexander had sought to simplify the problem by proposing that Jesus, as the Son of God, possessed eternal divinity, having always been of the same "substance" or essential nature as God the Father. However, one of his priests, Arius, countered by proposing that Christ, though ranking high above humanity, was nevertheless inferior to God and that his essential nature lay somewhere between the human and the divine. A bitter argument ensued that soon spread to other parts of the Roman Empire, with the result that in 325 CE, Emperor Constantine convened a council at Nicaea—an ancient city in what is now Turkey—in the hope of resolving the controversy. Athanasius, who in 328 succeeded Alexander as bishop of Alexandria, was the chief spokesman for Alexander's position, with Arius in attendance to promote his own view. Constantine, himself a Christian since 312, presided over the critical session at which a decision was made, and it was he who proposed the word *homoousios* (Greek for "of one essence") to describe Christ's relationship to God the Father. This term, of course, was compatible with Athanasius's position, and when the vote was taken only two bishops of the more than 200 present sided with Arius. Then, to exclude the possibility of future Arian error, the Council adopted the following creed:

> We believe in one God, the Father, Almighty, maker of all things visible and invisible;
>
> And in one Lord Jesus Christ, the Son of God, begotten of the Father, only-begotten, that is, from the substance {ousia} of the Father; God from God, Light from Light, Very God from Very God, begotten not made, of one substance {homoousios} with the Father, through whom all things were made, both in heaven and on earth; who for us men and for our salvation came down and was incarnate, was made man, suffered, and rose again on the third day, ascended into heaven, and is coming to judge the living and the dead;
>
> And in the Holy Spirit. . . .

(Later, at the Council of Constantinople in 381 CE, this creed was revised to create what is now called the "Nicene Creed," so-called because it originally had been formulated at the Council of Nicea. The "Athanasian Creed," quoted in part at the beginning of this chapter, was formulated in the late fourth or early fifth century with specific mention of the

Trinity. Although Athanasius did not write the creed, it bears his name probably because he was a strong proponent of the doctrine of the Trinity.)

The Council of Nicaea set a number of precedents, among them the power of the emperor to give quasi-legal status to the decisions of councils and the introduction of a new kind of orthodoxy that gave nonbiblical terms critical importance. The council, however, did not succeed in bringing theological unity to either the empire or the Christian church. With each new emperor exerting a different influence, any semblance of stability was usually short-lived. Moreover, Arianism continued to thrive, especially in the northern parts of Europe.

In the sixth century, however, the Byzantine emperor Justinian ("Justinian the Pious," he was called) went a long way toward establishing doctrinal uniformity by incorporating creedal beliefs, including that of the Trinity, into Roman law through the *Codex Justinianeus*. The universalist doctrines of Origen, the great theologian of Alexandria, were among those specifically condemned. Even though the empire had broken apart by this time, in many areas its laws nevertheless continued to be enforced. In addition, Emperor Justinian extended his rule from Constantinople (now Istanbul, Turkey) into what had been the western part of the Roman Empire. During the centuries that followed, the bishops of Rome (or popes, as they came to be called) consistently invoked the *Codex* and, whenever possible, enlisted the help of the civil authorities in its enforcement. Under the *Codex* the propagation of heretical views was judged to be a more serious crime than even murder, since it involved the fate of a person's immortal soul rather than that of one's temporal body. What little freedom of belief and tolerance that had managed to survive was now cut off; Christianity had become, not a faithful way of life, but a matter of doctrinal correctness.

Justinian's action did not bring a complete end to theological controversy, however. In the course of time, beginning in the fifth century, the Christian church, while affirming its own unity, had for all practical purposes separated into two divisions, one centered in Rome, the other in Constantinople. In the seventh century, a dispute arose between them over a seemingly minor point in the Nicene Creed. The Eastern, or Greek, church accused the Western, or Latin, church of having made an unauthorized change in the creed by affirming that the Holy Spirit comes not only from the Father, but from the Son as well. The disagreement came to be called the "*filioque* controversy," from the Latin phrase meaning "and the Son." The dispute, even over such a fine point of doctrine, grew increasingly bitter.

There were other divisive issues as well: the celibacy of the priesthood, the veneration of icons, the difference in language, even the church calendar, but the *filioque* controversy was a major factor leading to a final split between the two branches. In the eleventh century East and West went their separate ways—East as the Eastern Orthodox Church, West as the Roman Catholic Church. The Unitarian movement was to have its origins in the West.

Beginning in the late twelfth century, the Roman church attempted to ensure doctrinal correctness through the Inquisition, an institution designed to hunt out and punish Christians holding heretical views. A church-appointed inquisitor (or inquiror) would arrive suddenly in town and call for the identification of all those suspected of heresy. Those so identified were then summoned to appear before the inquisitor, who acted as prosecutor, judge, and jury, usually giving the accused no opportunity to confront their accusers or even learn their identity. Trials were held in private and sometimes went on for extended periods while the inquisitors used torture in an effort to extort confession. Pregnant women were exempt from torture, but only until after delivery. Penance following confession was sometimes light, depending on the inquisitor and the nature of the charge, and consisted of pilgrimages, fines, or required attendance at masses. However, in cases where the charges were more serious, the penalty might be the wearing of distinctive symbols, confiscation of property, or the loss of legal rights.

For those who were found guilty of the most serious heresies, such as denial of the Trinity, and who remained unrepentant, the penalties were severe, often death by burning at the stake. The stake, rather than the sword, was widely favored because of the church's opposition to the shedding of blood, and the punishment was often exacted by the civil rather than the ecclesiastical authorities because of the church's scruples against the taking of human life! The Inquisition became a powerful and dreaded force in Spain, France, and Italy for at least three centuries. In Spain, where it had been brought under royal control by King Ferdinand and Queen Isabella, the Grand Inquisitor Torquemada forced Moslems and Jews to either convert to Christianity or else be banished from the kingdom. As Columbus's ships were sailing off to find a new route to India, other ships were taking "infidels" into exile.

Even before these ships sailed off on their voyages of hope and despair, a new force for change was at work in Western European culture. The bleakness and intellectual poverty of the Middle Ages was being left behind, and a rebirth of literature, the arts, and science was taking place. The Renaissance, as this cultural rebirth was called, began with the revival of classical learning by scholars known as Humanists. The term "Humanist" originally had applied to teachers of Latin grammar, but its meaning gradually broadened to include all those who studied and based their philosophy on the Latin and Greek classics.

The development of Humanism and the growth of the Renaissance as a whole were greatly accelerated, and in part initiated, by Johann Gutenberg's invention of the printing press in the middle of the fifteenth century. Significantly, the first book Gutenberg published was the Bible, and it, too, quickly became an object of Humanist study. Up until then in the Roman church the study and interpretation of the Bible had been the province of the church's scholastic theologians, who applied Greek philosophy to the Bible and early Christian writings to develop their creedal systems. But now the situation changed radically; the Bible had become widely available, and in the new intellectual climate it was open to fresh interpretations. It was not long before the doctrine of the Trinity came under fresh scrutiny.

In 1516 (the year, incidentally, before the Reformation began), Erasmus of Rotterdam, considered the greatest of the Humanists, published a scholarly edition of the Greek New Testament that omitted the so-called *Comma Johanneum*, long cited as the Biblical proof text for the doctrine. The original text of 1 John 5:8 reads: "There are three on earth that bear witness: the Spirit, the water, and the blood, and these three agree as one." Erasmus discovered that at a later date there had been added the following: "There are three that bear record in Heaven: the Father, the Word, and the Holy Spirit, and these three are One." Moreover, the new intellectual climate helped to undermine the various arguments in support of the Trinity that scholastic theologians had developed over the years. It became evident that the doctrine had to be accepted strictly on faith or tradition, and this the vast majority of Humanists, themselves Christians, were willing to do. Nevertheless, the forces set loose by the Renaissance made a major reevaluation of the Roman church's faith and practice inevitable.

Matters were brought to a head on October 30, 1517, when Martin Luther posted ninety-five theses on the door of the church in Wittenberg, Germany. In so doing, the young monk had no thought of provoking a major controversy—he was simply hoping to promote a debate on what he saw as abuses in the Catholic Church's practice of granting indulgences, the means whereby a penitent sinner's time spent in purgatory could be shortened by paying money to the church. Nor was there anything new in the posting of theses on a church door; this was an established practice for initiating discussion of church matters. The theses were written in a moderate, academic tone (Luther was a professor of biblical studies at the newly founded University of Wittenberg), but their contents struck a raw nerve in the ecclesiastical hierarchy—not only were the practices he attacked well-established, but they were a significant source of income for the church. In the controversy that followed, Luther stood his ground, eventually challenging both the authority of the church and the supremacy of the pope. Excommunication came in 1521; by then the Reformation was well underway.

During the decade that followed, many Germans, including the Humanists, sided with Luther, who by then was advocating not only ecclesiastical reform, but theological reform as well. Luther built a theology based squarely on scripture, one that affirmed "the priesthood of all believers" and asserted that people are saved (or justified in the eyes of God), not by works, as the Church of Rome taught, but by faith alone. By 1526 his followers were beginning to organize churches based on these new doctrines, principally in Saxony, a region in northern Germany.

When at the Diet of Speyer in southwestern Germany three years later, Emperor Charles V attempted to curb the spread of the new movement, some of the princes of the German states stood up in protest; thus did the term "Protestant" originate. A year later, at the Diet of Augsburg, the Lutherans submitted their statement of belief, known as the Augsburg Confession, drafted by Luther's friend and confidant Philip Melanchthon; Luther himself was not permitted to be present. The Confession was a conciliatory document, stressing the elements held in common between Lutheranism and Catholicism; even the authority of the pope was not specifically rejected. However, the document affirmed Luther's doctrine of justification by faith and disavowed the Catholic dogma of transubstantiation, which held that in the eucharist, or communion, the bread and wine are miraculously converted into the body and blood of Christ, even though they still appear as bread and wine. Luther held that Christ was present in the bread and wine, but that they weren't transformed. A series of conferences followed, but in the end both emperor and pope found the statement unacceptable. The Lutherans, now firmly united, stood fast; by 1531 the breach was complete.

Meanwhile the religious leaven of the Renaissance was at work in Switzerland as well. There a popular young priest named Ulrich Zwingli, who had become increasingly alienated from the Roman church, quite independently concluded that the Bible should be the sole source of Christian truth. "I began to preach the gospel of Christ in the year 1516," he said, "before anyone in my locality had so much as heard the name of Luther." Zwingli and his followers, centered in the theocracy they were establishing in the city of Zürich, soon joined the Reformation movement.

However, Zwingli and Luther, who agreed to disagree on many points, came to unreconcilable differences regarding the eucharist: Luther insisted on the real presence of Christ in the bread and wine, while Zwingli insisted that they were to be understood only symbolically. As a result, Zwingli lost the crucial military support of the Lutheran princes; when in 1531 the five Catholic cantons (or states) in Switzerland sent an army against Zürich, he died in battle. Zwingli was a Humanist, greatly influenced by Erasmus, and the first of the Reformers to develop and publish a systematic theology, an ordered explanation of the central concepts of the Christian faith. His legacy was to persist, not only throughout the Reformation, but far beyond; among his heirs were the Puritans of New England, the ecclesiastical if not theological forerunners of American Unitarianism.

Elsewhere in Switzerland, at Geneva, a third leader of the Reformation emerged. John Calvin had become a Protestant as the result of a profound religious experience. As a young French scholar devoted to Humanist studies, he had suddenly experienced God speaking to him from the Bible, calling on him to mend his ways. "God subdued and brought my heart to docility," he reported. "It was more hardened against such matters than was to be expected in such a young man." Breaking with Roman Catholicism, he sought the freer religious climate of Switzerland. There in 1536, at the age of only twenty-seven, he published the first edition of his *Institutes of the Christian Religion*, the most influential theological treatise of the Reformation. He had hoped to devote his life to theological scholarship, but soon he was persuaded to assume leadership of the Reformation movement in Geneva. There, as will be related later, he was to play a major part in attempting to nip the Unitarian heresy in the bud.

Like Luther and Zwingli, Calvin based his theology exclusively on the interpretation of scripture, but it included two unique doctrines that ran contrary to Humanist thought: that of the innate sinfulness, even depravity, of humanity, and that of election, whereby only certain people were predestined for salvation, with the rest condemned to destruction. Centuries later, opposition to these doctrines would help give rise to Unitarianism and Universalism in America. As for the eucharist, Calvin contended that Christ was spiritually present to the elect, but absent to the nonelect. Like the other leading reformers, he initially showed only limited interest in the doctrine of the Trinity.

Unlike Luther, who retained many of the organizational and liturgical practices of Catholicism, Calvin attempted to place, not only his system of doctrine, but also his system of church organization and worship, on a firm biblical basis. The doctrines of human depravity and predestination that Calvin espoused characterize what came to be known as Calvinism. Churches on the European continent that adopted his theology and system of church governance are called Reformed; many such churches in the British Isles and North America became known as Presbyterian, named after the system of church governance rather than after the theology.

Not all those caught up in the ferment of the Reformation shared the zeal of Luther, Zwingli, and Calvin for ecclesiastical organization and the formulation of theological systems.

There were those—and their numbers were large—who were seeking a religious community of free spirits, one with no set standards of belief, little formal organization, and no prescribed forms of worship; instead they were seeking firsthand religious experience through direct communion with God. Though hard to define because of their diversity, these people became known as Anabaptists or re-baptizers, a name they never accepted but that described their one common belief, namely, that baptism should be reserved for those who as mature men and women had accepted Christ. Thus they contended that those who had been baptized as infants—the practice of the Roman Catholic Church—should be *re*-baptized, since their original baptism was without validity. The practice of re-baptizing, moreover, had long been condemned by the Catholic Church as a heresy punishable by death, an action originally designed to suppress the Donatists, a breakaway North African sect. It was among these Anabaptists that the Unitarian heresy (and, incidentally, the Universalist heresy as well) first broke out in the early years of the Reformation.

Anabaptism first emerged as an identifiable religious movement in 1525 when Zwingli's church in Zürich began to enforce the practice of infant baptism and banished the leaders of those who opposed it. The differences went far beyond the matter of baptism, however; Zwingli was determined to build a state church, while the Anabaptists wanted a church completely free from state control. Many Anabaptists soon migrated to Germany, where their ranks were swelled by disgruntled peasants whose insurrection against the established social order had just been violently suppressed. Many of these newcomers were more interested in radical social change than in religious reform, and for several decades thereafter the movement was viewed as a major threat by Catholics, Reformers, and civil authorities alike. The threat was considered so serious that the Diet of Speyer in 1529 issued a death decree against all Anabaptists. Following a bloody uprising by the Anabaptists in the city of Münster in 1535, thousands through-

out the region were put to death, either by drowning, beheading, or burning. The leaders of the uprising were horribly
tortured and executed, and their bodies were suspended in
cages from a church tower, where they remained until 1881!
The Anabaptist movement managed to survive, however, under new and more moderate leadership; it remained a significant religious and social force in Germany, Holland, and
England throughout the remainder of the sixteenth century.

While the majority of Anabaptists had little interest in
doctrinal questions and those that did held a variety of opinions, there were a number of individuals among them who, in
the early years of the Reformation, had thought their way
through to antitrinitarian positions; they thus can be thought
of as forerunners of the Unitarian movement. Most of these
forerunners paid a high price for making their views known—
they were either exiled, imprisoned, or executed.

The first Protestant to openly oppose the Trinity was Martin Cellarius, who in 1527 published a small volume, *De
operabis Dei (Concerning the Workings of God)*. In this work
Cellarius claimed in passing that Jesus was God because he
shared fully in the deity that dwelt within him and in the Holy
Spirit, which he had without measure; Cellarius further claimed
that "we are *all* gods and sons of the Most High through
sharing in this same deity and Spirit." Although Cellarius
embraced Anabaptist views, quarreled with Luther, and spent
a short time in prison, he was a respected scholar, and his
moderate style of expression doubtless saved him from more
severe punishment. A generation later his book was to become
highly regarded in Transylvania by those in the fledgling
Unitarian movement there. He died in 1564 at the age of sixty-
five, a victim of the plague, a fate not uncommon to the times.

A more significant figure was Johann Denck, regarded as
the most important of the German Anabaptists. A gifted scholar,
teacher, and missionary, his views were widely accepted in the
Rhine cities, as well as in Franconia, Bavaria, Switzerland, and
Moravia. One's religious experience, he asserted, constitutes a

continuous revelation of God, more basic than either scripture or tradition. Moreover, he taught that the true church is not an external organization composed of those who accept a common creed, but is rather a spiritual fellowship of all those in whom God's Spirit dwells. Further, like numerous other Anabaptists, he believed in universal salvation.

Predictably, Denck's views brought him into frequent conflict with the Lutherans, who hounded him from one city to another. Several of his opponents accused him of being an antitrinitarian, and, indeed, in one of his tracts he stated that the only Trinity of God consists of omnipotence, goodness, and righteousness. Even though Denck's active leadership was limited to just three years, his influence on the Anabaptist movement was enormous; that influence was not great enough, however, for him to bring organization to the movement or to reverse its trend toward extremism. He died in 1528 at the age of thirty-two, like Cellarius a victim of the plague.

One of Denck's co-workers, Ludwig Haetzer, left less doubt as to where he stood theologically, openly denying the orthodox Catholic doctrines of the Trinity, vicarious atonement (that Christ died for the sins of humanity), and eternal punishment. A hymn he wrote is quite specific about his view of the Godhead.

> I am He who created all things through His own might.
> Thou askest, how many persons am I?
> I am one!
> I am not three persons, but I am one!
> And I cannot be three persons, for I am one!
> I know nothing of persons: I alone am the source of
> all life.
> Him who doth not know me, I know not;
> I alone am!

Haetzer, like Denck a gifted scholar, denied in writing the deity of Christ, holding that Christ was neither equal to God nor of one essence with the Father; because of Zwingli's opposition, however, his manuscript was never published and later was destroyed. Like Denck, Haetzer found himself driven from city to city because of his heretical views. In the end he was beheaded, not for heresy, however, but for sexual immorality, a charge frequently leveled against the Anabaptists at that time.

Not surprisingly, the antitrinitarian views of Anabaptists such as Denck and Haetzer were quite specifically repudiated in the Augsburg Confession, the Lutheran statement of belief. The future of Lutheranism and of the Reformation itself was hanging in the balance, and Melanchthon and Luther's other supporters were anxious to put as much distance as possible between them and such radical views.

One other Anabaptist deserves mention because his extremism illustrates the doctrinal ferment of the times. In 1530, the very year of the Augsburg Confession, Conradin Bassin was arrested at Basel in Switzerland for preaching not only that Christ was neither God nor Savior, but also his disbelief in the New Testament, prayer, and a future life. Refusing to recant, he was beheaded, his head impaled, and his body burned.

Meanwhile, Anabaptists were making their way to Holland, where Lutheranism was weak and the religious climate thought to be more tolerant. Among these migrants was Melchior Hofmann, who quickly rose to leadership as his persuasive preaching won many converts. Soon, however, his preaching became dominated by his conviction that he was the biblical prophet Elijah, sent to proclaim that the end of the world was nigh and the millenium at hand (the thousand-year reign of Christ on earth). His message spread rapidly throughout the desperate and impoverished underclasses of Holland and Germany, helping to precipitate the 1535 Anabaptist uprising at Münster. By then Hofmann had returned to Germany, been arrested, tried, and sentenced to life imprisonment. At his trial he had denied both the divinity and humanity of Christ and claimed that prayer should be offered only to God the Father. After the Münster debacle, the persecution of the Anabaptists quickly spread to Holland, where by 1546 some 30,000 had been put to death. Eventually the chastened survivors were organized under the moderating influence of Menno Simons into a stable, law-abiding religious body. They became known as Mennonites, as are their spiritual descendants today.

While none of the antitrinitarian Anabaptists properly qualify as pioneers of the Unitarian movement—they were in no way directly connected with it either institutionally or through their teachings—they nevertheless bore witness in a unique way to its principles of freedom, reason, and tolerance. They were instead pioneers of their own movement, connected historically down through the years with the Baptists, Mennonites, Church of the Brethren, and others. Historically the two movements have shared much in common—congregational polity, broad individual freedom of belief, an emphasis on religious living rather than on creeds, advocacy of church-state separation, and a strong commitment to peace—but they have been, and remain, two distinct, separate movements.

When Michael Servetus's book, *On the Errors of the Trinity*, appeared in 1531, the Anabaptist movement was already underway, and the Unitarian movement not yet begun. Any antitrinitarian utterances from Anabaptist sources could be discounted readily as coming from a radical fringe movement, quite beyond the pale—a movement to be suppressed at all costs, not because of the utterances of a few of its members, but because of its commitment to overturn the whole religious and social order. On the other hand, Servetus's book presented quite another problem. The author, though young, was obviously an able scholar, untarred by the brush of Anabaptism. His book, moreover, was raising questions that the leaders of the Reformation would have preferred to have left unasked. Certainly what they did *not* need was a divisive debate over a doctrine that the Roman church held sacred, especially after their conciliatory statement just made at Augsburg. Little wonder, then, that Philip Melanchthon, after reading Servetus's book, would write, "As for the Trinity, you know I have always feared this would break out some day. Good God, what tragedies this question will excite . . . !"

The Life and Death of Michael Servetus

If you find me in error in one point you should not on that account condemn me in all, for according to this there is no mortal who would not be burned a thousand times, for we know in part. . . . Such is human frailty that we condemn the spirits of others as impostors and impious and except our own, for no one recognizes his own errors. . . . I beg you, for God's sake, to spare my name and fame.

—MICHAEL SERVETUS TO JOHANNES OECOLAMPADIUS

$\mathcal{W}$hen *On the Errors of the Trinity* appeared in 1531, Michael Servetus had barely entered his twenties. He had been brought up in the Aragonian village of Villanueva, at the foot of the Spanish Pyrenees, a member of a well-established, devout, and respected Catholic family. His father was a nobleman, his brother Juan a priest. When Michael was fifteen or sixteen, his father sent him across the mountains into France to study law at the University of Toulouse. It was there that Servetus first encountered the Bible and immediately became fascinated by its contents. Up until then whatever religious instruction he had received had been speculative and abstract, but as he studied the New Testament the figure of Jesus came alive to him in a forceful, concrete way. Moreover, to his amazement, he could find in it "not one word about the Trinity, nor about its Persons, nor about an Essence, nor about a unity of the Substance, nor about one Nature of the several beings." Given the importance of such matters to both his church and his country, young Servetus found such omissions perplexing.

It had been only a generation earlier that hundreds of thousands of Jews and Moslems had been banished from Spain, or in some cases put to death, for their refusal to accept the doctrine of the Trinity and convert to Christianity. Many *had* converted when faced with this choice, but the motives of these *conversos* were suspect, and they often found themselves under surveillance and called by the insulting name of *Marranos* (which means "swine"). Throughout the rest of Western Europe there was a widespread feeling that these forced conversions had badly compromised the Christian faith throughout Spain—in Martin Luther's view, it was preferable to have a Turk for an enemy than a Spaniard for a protector. "The Spaniards are all *Marranos*," he said, "and, whereas other heretics defend their opinions obstinately, the *Marranos* shrug their shoulders and hold nothing for certain." Predictably, both the Spanish church and monarchy were deeply offended by such opinions—for them, the very honor of their country and their church was at stake.

Given such a climate, young Servetus was deeply disturbed that he had found no direct statement in the Bible supporting such a central doctrine; nor was the key word *homoousios*, describing the relationship of the Father to the Son, to be found there either. To be sure, there were references to Father, Son, and Holy Spirit, but nowhere was it asserted that the three were one. Should, then, acceptance of such an unscriptural doctrine be required of Jews and Moslems? How did the doctrine arise? How could it be clarified? In his search for answers, he began to study diligently the Bible and the Church Fathers (the writers of the first centuries of the Christian church who established what came to be considered orthodox Christian doctrine).

His studies were interrupted, however, when he was called back to Spain into the service of Juan de Quintana, the Confessor to Emperor Charles V. Charles, for political reasons, was going to Italy so that Pope Clement VII could crown him emperor of the Holy Roman Empire. Young Servetus sailed from Spain with the royal entourage in 1529, never to return. Since Charles had already been crowned ten years before by nonpapal hands, the coronation was something akin to having a church wedding after a civil ceremony has already taken place. Nevertheless, it turned out to be a magnificent spectacle, full of pomp and pageantry. A great procession made its way through the thronged streets of Bologna, with the pope, a triple crown on his head, riding amid four cardinals walking on foot. Then, seated on a golden chair under a golden canopy, he received the emperor, who kissed his feet in obeisance. Servetus, fresh from his study of the Bible, was revolted. Some twenty years later he was to write with anger and disgust:

> With these very eyes we have seen him [the pope] borne in pomp on the neck of princes, making with his hands the sign of the cross, and adored in the open streets by all the people on bended knee, so that those who were able to kiss his feet or slippers counted themselves more fortunate than the rest, and declared that they had obtained many indulgences, and that on this account the infernal pains would be remitted for many years. O vilest of all beasts, most brazen of harlots!

It was a defining experience; Servetus had become a Reformer, committed to the restoration of Christianity, both its doctrines and its institutions.

Soon after the coronation, Servetus made his way northward to Protestant soil; there he not only would be safer in expressing his now rapidly developing views, but also might convert others to these views. It is possible that he accompanied Quintana and the emperor to the Diet of Augsburg, called to attempt a reconciliation of the differences between Rome and the Reformers; if he did, he may have encountered Philip Melanchthon and other leading Reformers at first hand. At any rate, at some point he discreetly slipped away from the imperial retinue and made his way to Basel, in Switzerland, where he lived for some months at the home of Johannes Oecolampadius, the city's leading Reformer. It was at Basel, during the latter half of 1530 and the early months of 1531, that he wrote the text of *De Trinitatis Erroribis* (or, in English, *On the Errors of the Trinity*).

Despite his youth, Servetus, a product of the Renaissance, was already amazingly well-read at the time he undertook this task, quite at home in Hebrew, Greek, and Latin. Not only the Bible, but the writings of the early Church Fathers, provided grist for his mill as he struggled to replace the traditional understanding of the Trinity with a sounder, richer, more biblical one. The traditional understanding, he claimed, was abstract, sterile, lifeless, philosophically unsound, and leading to three gods rather than one. It was imperative, he believed, that the relationships between Father, Son, Holy Spirit, and *Logos* be reexamined in a biblical light. In a sense, Servetus was and remained a trinitarian; it was an erroneous understanding of the relationships that he opposed and was striving to correct.

Gradually the new understanding that he sought began taking shape in Servetus's mind. One thing had been clear to him: that Jesus was a man; further, that any understanding of Christ must depend on an understanding of the relationship between humanity and God. Those who made a sharp distinction between humanity and God, he said, "do not understand the nature of humanity, which is of such a character that God can communicate to it divinity, . . . not by a degradation of divinity but by an exaltation of humanity. . . . God sends to us his light and this is God himself. . . . I say, therefore, that God himself is our spirit dwelling in us, and this is the Holy Spirit within us." This was not, however, to deny the special character of Christ:

> If you say [wrote Servetus] that you can see no difference between Christ and the others, since we are all called sons of God, I answer that if we are called sons of

God it is simply through His [Christ's] gift and his grace, for He is the author of our sonship, and so is called Son in a more excellent way. That is why the article is used and Christ is called *the* Son of God, to show that he is not a son in a general sense as we are, but in a very special and peculiar sense. He is a natural Son. Others are not born but become sons of God. By faith in Christ we are made sons of God, therefore by adoption we are called sons.

For Servetus the *Logos* (the "Word" of God, or a divine principle regulating all things) was eternal, a mode of God's self-expression, ever-latent in God's very being. This *Logos* became incarnate in the man Jesus, thereby making Jesus the Son of God. The *Logos*, then, was eternal, the Son not eternal. Servetus admitted a Trinity of dispensations or modes of God's activity, for there is one God who manifests Himself in diverse ways. For example, "the Holy Spirit is not a distinct Being," said Servetus, it is simply God's spirit moving within our hearts. Thus, too, is the one God manifested in Christ. Quite independently, Servetus was restating the old Sabellian or modalist heresy, which had claimed that God existed in three different modes. Moreover, just as there had been a time when there was no mediator between humanity and God, there would come a time when a mediator would become unnecessary. "The Kingdom of Christ is a thousand times called eternal. Yet in the consummation of the ages He shall restore it to God. . . . [Then] every ministry of the Holy Spirit shall cease since we shall no longer need an advocate or mediator because God will be All-in-all. Then, also, the Trinity of dispensation will terminate." Through all of this, Servetus's thought was permeated by a profound sense that the new life in Christ is a life in which men and women live, not their *own* life, but one in which God, through God's spirit, lives in them.

Confident that he had found the truth, Servetus tried to press his views on Oecolampadius, who at first treated him with tolerance. In time, though, the older man's patience grew thin; as the leading Reformer of the city, he was in no mood to be instructed by some callow youth with decidedly unorthodox opinions. Particularly upsetting were Servetus's notions that the Son was not eternal and that the time would come when a mediator was no longer necessary. Eventually he gave vent to his growing frustration by writing to Servetus:

> You complain that I am too harsh. I have good reason. You contend that the Church of Christ for a great span has departed from the foundation of her faith. You accord more honor to Tertullian [one of the early Church Fathers] than to the whole Church. You deny the one person in two natures. By denying that the Son is eternal you deny of necessity also that the Father is eternal. You have submitted a confession of faith which the simple and unsuspecting might approve, but I abominate your subterfuges. . . . I will be patient in other matters but when Christ is blasphemed, No!

Not long afterward, at a conference of leading Swiss Reformers, Oecolampadius warned the others about the young Spaniard's heresies. Ulrich Zwingli, in particular, was deeply concerned. It was imperative, he felt, that this heretic be either converted or silenced, lest the whole movement for reform be undermined. Sure of his views, but unsure of his safety, Servetus, manuscript in hand, departed Basel for the German city of Strassburg (now Strasbourg), a place well known for its tolerance. It was the home of Mathias Zell and his wife Catherine ("Catherine, the Intrepid," she was called), a couple renowned for their devotion to religious liberty. In addition, both the magistrates and clergy of the city were disinclined to interfere with religious expression; hence Anabaptists and members of other unorthodox groups had found a haven there. It seemed a good place from which to promulgate one's views.

It was time, Servetus decided, to promulgate his views in print, confident that when the Reformers had had an opportunity to study them, they would be converted to his position. In the nearby village of Hagenau he found a printer, Johannes Setzer, who was willing to undertake the task. Thus in the summer of 1531, *On the Errors of the Trinity* came off the press and went on sale, first at Strassburg, then at Basel, Bern, and elsewhere. It was a book of 238 pages, written in Latin and made up of seven parts. The first contained Servetus's main points; the last six were mostly commentary but included an attack on Luther's doctrine of justification by faith. Setzer probably risked publishing the book in order to irritate the Swiss Reformers, with whom he disagreed on points of doctrine; he was, however, cautious enough to omit from the book both his name and the place of publication.

Servetus's hopes of converting others through the printed word were dashed in short order. Erasmus refused the copy that was pressed upon him; Malanchthon became increasingly critical; Oecolampadius quickly had the book banned in Basel; Zwingli, soon to die in battle, predictably denounced it; so, too, did Martin Luther, probably without having read it; John Calvin, who was to become its most virulent critic, was still in Paris, his conversion experience several years away. After an initial favorable reception in Strassburg, the book was denounced there, too, and its sale prohibited. Within a year Protestant condemnation was well nigh universal. Disappointed and alarmed by this reception, Servetus rushed into print a second book, *Two Dialogues on the Trinity*. In it he confessed that the earlier book had been the product of immature thinking, and he attempted to restate his position in more acceptable and conciliatory terms. But other than modifying his criticism of Luther's doctrine of justification by faith (a minor theme, at best), his main points with respect to the doctrine of the Trinity, though disguised in new language, remained essentially unchanged; so, too, did the judgment of the Protestant Reformers.

In most of western Europe, Roman Catholic reaction to *On the Errors of the Trinity* was slow to develop. Not so in Spain. Servetus had been bold enough to send a copy across the Pyrenees to the bishop of Saragossa, and the reaction of the Spaniards, already hypersensitive on the subject, was immediate and strong. Quintana was outraged that a Spaniard, especially one who had been in his service, would have written such a despicable book. Predictably, the Inquisition, still on the lookout for heretics, was quick to move into action. "We deem it expedient," stated the inquisitors, "to try every possible means to lure [Servetus] back to Spain, enticing him by promises or other offers, and if this fail then exert pressure. . . . Let this be done with secrecy and despatch as the importance of the case requires." His own brother Juan was recruited for this mission, with instructions to locate the heretic and bring him back for trial; under the circumstances family loyalty was a poor second to one's loyalty to church and country. Soon Servetus was wanted by the Inquisition in Toulouse as well. Condemned by Catholics and Protestant Reformers alike and welcome nowhere, he even considered escaping to the New World so recently discovered by Columbus. A decade later he was to write:

> Knowing that I was young, powerless, and without polish of style, I almost gave up the whole cause, for I was not yet sufficiently trained. . . . O most clement Jesus, I invoke thee again as divine witness that on this account I delayed and also because of the imminent persecution, so that with Jonah I longed rather to flee to the sea or to one of the New Isles.

Rather than fleeing to the sea or the New Isles, Michael Servetus decided to go underground, leaving no trace of his whereabouts. It was rumored that he had gone mad and died in some old castle dungeon. Adopting the name of Michel de Villeneuve, he went first to Paris, where he arranged a meeting with John Calvin, then failed to keep the appointment. But the climate in the city was dangerous for non-Catholics and both men soon left—Servetus (or de Villeneuve) for Lyons, Calvin for Switzerland; it would be almost twenty years before the two would finally meet. Lyons was safer than Paris—the civil and ecclesiastical authorities were less rigorous in ferreting out heretics—and it was here and in the neighboring town of Vienne that Servetus spent most of the next two decades. He supported himself chiefly as an editor, soon earning a reputation for his skill and dependability; his most notable contributions were two editions of Ptolemy's *Geography* and a seven-volume edition of the *Santes Pagnini Bible.*

Servetus did return to Paris in 1536 for a two-year period in order to study medicine at the university there. He supported himself partly through his writing; his pharmaceutical monograph *On Syrups* went through six editions. At one point, cited before an inquisitor for his views on astrology, he chose to conduct his own defense, even though he risked being sent to the stake if his true identity became known. ("What nerve!" comments modern historian Roland Bainton.) He received only a relatively light reprimand. The most important result of his studies was his elucidation of the pulmonary circulation of blood, which he waited some fifteen years to report. For this discovery alone, Michael Servetus deserves a place in history. Whether he actually received a degree is uncertain—he had had a major quarrel with the dean—but thereafter he always claimed the title Doctor of Medicine.

Servetus left Paris in 1538 and busied himself with both editing and the practice of medicine, but his preoccupation with theology, though kept secret, remained very much alive. Back in 1532, "young, powerless, and without polish of style," he had almost given up "the whole cause," being "not yet sufficiently trained," but by 1546 he felt ready to enter the theological lists again, even if he kept his identity secret. A new book was taking shape in his mind and on paper. It was to be called *Christianismi Restitutio* (or in English, *The Restora-*

tion of Christianity). Much of the contents of his first book would be incorporated into the new one, but the impact of two new influences would become obvious. The first of these was a form of Neo-Platonism to which Servetus had been exposed during his years in France (Neo-Platonism teaches that the world has emanated from a single primal source, with which the soul can be reunited through mystical experience). The second influence was Anabaptism, to which he had been exposed during his stay in Strassburg. Neo-Platonism led Servetus to revise his understanding of God; Anabaptism led him to a rejection of infant baptism and reinforced his commitment to the restoration of primitive Christianity, or Christianity as it had been practiced in its first century.

Servetus's refined understanding of God has been well summarized by Earl Morse Wilbur, who wrote long before gender-inclusive language was being applied to the deity:

> His [new] doctrine of God is very noble: the mind fails when thinking of him, for he is incomprehensible, invisible, inaudible, intangible, ineffable, immeasurable, transcending all things, above all light, being spirit, or any object of thought. Hence he can be known only through the ways in which he has chosen to manifest himself to us, through eternal wisdom, through the word that he has uttered, through Christ, through created things. For he fills all things, on earth and even in hell. It is his presence in them that gives them their existence. God creates nothing to which he does not present and communicate himself. He is everywhere, the complete essence of all things. He so contains in himself the essence of all things that by his essence alone, without another creature, he can here manifest himself as fire, as air, as stone, as amber, as a twig, as a flower, as whatever else you will.

While this was not exactly pantheism as his critics often

claimed—Servetus was not identifying God with the created universe as pantheism does, but rather positing the universe as being a manifestation of God—it certainly represented an even further departure from traditional trinitarian theology than had his earlier writings. True, he still made room for Christ and the Holy Spirit, but both were clearly overshadowed by his grand vision of God as the ultimate source and creator of all things.

In giving his *magnum opus* the title *The Restoration of Christianity*, Servetus was siding with the Anabaptists against the leading Reformers; for while Luther, Zwingli, and Calvin were attempting to *reform* the sixteenth-century Christian church, the Anabaptists were attempting to *restore* primitive Christianity in actual congregations. A major part of this restoration involved the rejection of infant baptism and the reinstitution of the baptism of those adults who were open to regeneration. The church was to be a community of those who had repented of their sins and been reborn into a new life in Christ; infants, and indeed children and youths, were incapable of such repentance and rebirth. In this, of course, the Anabaptists were in direct conflict both with the Catholics and with the leading Reformers.

Servetus, while seeing the church as a *spiritual* community rather than one manifest in concrete form, had in other respects come to what was essentially an Anabaptist position. Children, he maintained, are born innocent and, like Adam, are incapable of either their best or worst until they have tasted the fruit of the tree of knowledge. Rather than being baptized, children should be dedicated with a prayer that God protect and preserve them until they become ready for spiritual rebirth. Following the example of Christ, baptism preferably should be postponed until the thirtieth year. For Servetus, as for the Anabaptists, the practice of infant baptism was at the very heart of the Catholic Church's corruption in that it took away the sacrament whereby men and women might be born again. "Woe, woe to you baptizers of babies," he was to write, "who have shut the Kingdom of Heaven to men, into which you do not enter nor suffer us to enter! Woe! woe!"

Just as he had fifteen years earlier, Servetus sought an influential Reformer whom he might convert to his position. Basel, Zürich, Wittenberg, and Strassburg were all closed to him, but an important new center of Protestantism had arisen at Geneva, with John Calvin as its leader. Servetus, writing under a pseudonym (undoubtedly that of Michel de Villeneuve), initiated a correspondence with Calvin, without appreciating how great a theological gulf lay between them. Nevertheless, Calvin at first responded courteously and at length, perhaps hoping to persuade Servetus of the error of his beliefs. However, as Servetus persisted in trying to instruct him on matters of Christology and baptism, Calvin lost patience, replying that his own views were already well formulated in his *Institutes of the Christian Religion*, a copy of which he enclosed; when it was returned with insulting annotations, he did not deign to reply. Servetus nevertheless persisted in sending more and more of his writings, including a draft manuscript of his new book. Calvin, who by then had discovered his correspondent's identity, had had enough. "Servetus," he wrote a friend, "has just sent me, together with his letters, a long volume of his ravings. If I consent he will come here, but I will not give my word, for should he come, if my authority is of any avail, I will not suffer him to get out alive." Servetus wrote again, requesting the return of the manuscript; again, John Calvin did not reply.

It was time, Servetus decided, to publish. He had retained a second copy of the manuscript; all that he needed was a printer. At length he found one in Lyons who was willing to undertake the task provided that it be conducted with the utmost secrecy. Neither author nor printer were to be identified, and the pages of the manuscript were burned as soon as they had been set in type. The publication of 1,000 copies of *The Restoration of Christianity* was completed early in 1553. Most were temporarily stored in Lyons, but some were sent to

Frankfurt and others to Geneva. There a copy came into the hands of Guillaume Trie, a fanatical Protestant and a close friend of Calvin. Trie had a Catholic cousin living in Lyons to whom he promptly wrote, chiding him because his church was permitting a heretic to live unpunished in its midst.

[A]lthough we allow greater liberty in religion and doctrine [he wrote], we do not suffer the name of God to be blasphemed. . . . I can give you an example which is greatly to your confusion. . . . You suffer a heretic, who well deserves to be burned wherever he may be. . . . [H]ere is one who will call Jesus Christ an idol, who will destroy all the fundamentals of the faith, who will amass all the phantasies of the ancient heretics, who will even condemn infant baptism, calling it an invention of the devil. And this man is in good repute among you, and is suffered as if he were not wrong. Where is the zeal you pretend? Where is the police of this fine hierarchy of which you so boast? The man of whom I speak has been condemned by all the churches you reprove, yet you suffer him and even let him print his books which are so full of blasphemies that I need say no more. He is a Portuguese Spaniard, named Michael Servetus. That is his real name, but he goes under the name of Villeneuve and practices medicine. Now he is at Vienne where his book has been printed by a certain Balthazar Arnoulette, and lest you think that I am talking without warrant I send you the first folio. . . . Geneva, Feb. 26.

That Servetus was the author of *The Restoration of Christianity* was quite evident in Geneva; copies of the letters that he had sent to Calvin were included as an appendix, and at one point in the book's text there is a dialogue in which one interlocutor says to the other, "I perceive that you are Servetus." Servetus had been confident that, though he might be in jeopardy on Protestant soil, he would be quite safe in France, where, as Michel de Villeneuve, Doctor of Medicine, he had a circle of distinguished friends and was by all outward appearances a faithful Roman Catholic. What he had not counted on was the possibility that his identity would be disclosed to the Catholic Church by the Protestants themselves.

Trie's cousin promptly placed the letter and the enclosed folio in the hands of the local inquisitor, and by mid-March, "Michel de Villeneuve" had been summoned to appear before an informal group of judges to answer their questions. Servetus was slow to arrive—apparently he was destroying any incriminating evidence—but when he finally appeared, he welcomed a search of his premises. Nothing was found. The judges then questioned Arnoullet, the printer identified in Trie's letter, without result. Stymied, the judges had a letter written to Trie, requesting the full text of the book. Trie replied promptly:

> . . . I cannot for the moment give you what you want, namely the printed book. But I can give you something better to convict him, namely two dozen manuscript pieces of the man in question, in which his heresies are in part contained. If you show him the printed book he can deny it, which he cannot do in respect of his handwriting. . . . I can tell you I had no little trouble to get from Calvin what I am sending. Not that he does not wish to repress such execrable blasphemies, but he thinks his duty is rather to convince heretics with doctrine than with other means, because he does not exercise the sword of justice. . . . From Geneva on the last day of March.

Whatever qualms John Calvin may have had, the fact remains that it was he who supplied the damning evidence to the Roman Catholic Inquisition.

On April 4, 1553, the inquisitor presented the evidence to the cardinal, archbishop, and vicars of the region, together with other officials and theologians. It was agreed that Servetus and Arnoullet should be arrested and brought to trial. Servetus was cross-examined at length on both April 5 and 6. Early on the morning of April 7, in bathrobe and nightcap, he prevailed upon the jailer to let him go out into the jail's walled garden to relieve himself. Doffing his robe and nightcap, Servetus, fully dressed, escaped over the wall; a careful search failed to disclose his whereabouts. The trial continued without him, and on June 17, sentence was passed. He was found guilty *in absentia* of heresy, sedition, rebellion, and evasion of prison and condemned to be burned at the stake. On December 23 the sentence was carried out; Michael Servetus was burned in effigy together with copies of his book, many of which had been discovered stored in Lyons. Meanwhile, Arnoullet, before eventually being released from prison, had managed to get word to a friend to destroy the copies that had been sent to Frankfurt. The destruction of Servetus's *magnum opus* was so complete that, of the thousand copies printed, only three survive.

"On August the 13th of the present year [1553] Michael Servetus was recognized by certain brothers and it seemed good to make him a prisoner that he might no longer infect the world with his heresies, seeing that he was known to be incorrigible and hopeless"—thus reads the record of the Genevan Consistory (the ruling body of Calvin's church). August 13 was a Sunday, and Servetus was in church as part of his plan "to keep himself hid as much as he could," for *not* being in church would have brought suspicion on anyone in Geneva in those days. But "certain brothers from Lyons" spotted him in the congregation and reported him to Calvin. He was arrested and imprisoned at once, never to see freedom again.

There has been much speculation as to why Servetus went to Geneva in the first place. Perhaps he wished to make common cause with the Libertines, a political group that strongly opposed Calvin's iron-hand rule of the city and that was struggling to gain control. Perhaps it was to seek his own death as part of an apocalyptic vision that the end of the age was at hand. More likely it was for the reason that he later gave at his trial: that he was simply passing through on his way to Naples, where he planned to practice medicine.

Genevan law required that both the accused and the accuser be promptly imprisoned until the authorities could determine whether the accusation was justified; if it was not, then the accuser must suffer the penalty for the crime that had been charged. Since Calvin, the accuser, was virtual dictator of the city, in charge of both civil and ecclesiastical matters, he was able to arrange to have a substitute imprisoned in his place. The law also required that the accused should be given the opportunity to respond to the charges against him within twenty-four hours of arrest; hence Calvin hurriedly went through Servetus's writings, identifying thirty-eight charges to be brought against him. These his surrogate accuser, Nicolas de la Fontaine, presented in a preliminary hearing conducted the following day by an assistant prosecutor. Servetus answered the charges one by one, admitting some, denying others, and giving qualified answers to yet others. After de la Fontaine had attempted to refute Servetus's replies, the two were returned to prison.

On the following day the assistant prosecutor reported to the city's Council, which voted to continue the case. Servetus was examined again on the same charges and again answered them, this time more fully. The charges were concerned primarily with Servetus's early life, his writings, and his beliefs about the Trinity, pantheism, immortality, and baptism. He was accused of being a troublemaker in his earlier years, which he denied, and of being the author of *On the Errors of the Trinity*, a book that had "infected many people"; Servetus admitted the book's authorship, but denied its infectious qualities. As for beliefs, he defended his views on the Trinity, repudiated the charges of being a pantheist and of denying immortality, and admitted without reservation his condemnation of infant baptism.

The Council was now satisfied that the charges against him

had substance, and de la Fontaine was released from custody and instructed to present evidence on the following day in support of his case. Germain Colladon, one of Calvin's confidential friends, was chosen to represent de la Fontaine as prosecutor for the next day's proceedings, doubtless at Calvin's request. At the same time, and to Calvin's displeasure, a Libertine, Philibert Berthelier, entered the case as the representative of the state. The entry of these two men into the proceedings brought into sharp relief the power struggle going on in the city: Berthelier had been fighting to have removed a ban of excommunication imposed on him by Calvin, while Calvin had been saying that he would rather die a hundred deaths than to permit this to happen.

The session with Colladon and Berthelier was brief but stormy, and when the trial resumed the next day (it was by then August 17), Calvin himself had assumed the role of prosecutor to maintain control of the situation. Servetus's editorial notes in the *Pagnini Bible* and Ptolemy's *Geography* were examined, as were, once again, his views on the Trinity. It was a distorted doctrine that he had attacked, Servetus claimed, one that destroyed the unity of God, and it was such an idea of God that he had, in fact, called a three-headed Cerberus (the name of a three-headed dog that guards the entrance to the world of the dead in Greek and Roman mythology). Calvin, relentless in his cross-examination, succeeded in convincing the Council that the trial should move on to a next step. Three days later he wrote to Guillaume Farel, his close friend and fellow Reformer: "I hope he [Servetus] will at least be sentenced to death, though it is my wish that he be spared needless cruelty." To which Farel replied that for Calvin to spare Servetus cruelty would amount to showing friendship to his worst enemy.

During a ten-day interval before the trial was resumed, Calvin and his fellow ministers held a meeting with Servetus to refute the interpretation of the early Church Fathers that he had used in his writings. According to Calvin, the ministers were prepared to discuss the matter quietly and objectively, but Servetus heaped so many insults on them that no useful discussion was possible. Perhaps Berthelier's earlier appearance as the representative of the state had given him an unwarranted sense of confidence; indeed, Servetus seems to have expected throughout the trial that the Libertines would somehow intercede on his behalf. The ministers did agree to supply him with books, paper, and pen with which to prepare his defense; they also instructed the prison guards that henceforth he be held *incommunicado*.

During this same interval the Council sent a letter to the Catholic court in Vienne, asking for documents and other evidence that the court had used in its trial of Servetus some months earlier. The Council soon received a polite reply, denying this request and asking instead that the prisoner be returned, so that his death sentence could be carried out. The Vienne court also requested that Servetus attest to the fact that the jailor had not helped him to escape. This Servetus gladly did, but when asked whether he wished to be returned to Vienne, he fell to his knees in tears and begged that the trial be continued in Geneva. On that same day he petitioned the Council on three counts: first, that he be set free, since religious questions historically had been settled in church courts, not in those of the state, and that the maximum penalty for heresy traditionally had been banishment; second, that he should not be charged with any crime against the state, since he never had been guilty of sedition or disturbing the peace and always had opposed the Anabaptists' attitude toward civil government; and third, that since he was a stranger in the city and ignorant of its customs, he should be given legal council. His petition was rejected on all counts.

Meanwhile, both de la Fontaine and Colladon had been relieved of any further involvement in the case, and prosecution had been placed in the hands of the state's attorney-general, Claude Rigot. Rigot prepared a whole new set of charges to replace those originally brought by Calvin through de la Fontaine. Those had been speculative and theological in nature; the new ones were practical, stressing the destructive effects of heresy on the social order and public morality. These effects, moreover, could be shown to be evident in the life of Servetus himself. Whether Calvin was directly involved in drawing up these new charges is uncertain, but the following Sunday he preached on the subject to a crowded congregation.

When the trial was resumed the attorney-general questioned Servetus closely on his sexual life (his replies indicated that because of a rupture and an operation he had had little, if any), on his writings (he had not thought that they would upset Christendom), and on his presumed sympathy with Moslems and Jews (he had had little contact with either and thought the Koran a bad book; these last questions were prompted by a belief widely held at the time that tolerance of Servetus's views would lead to an Islamic takeover of Europe). On the whole, during this portion of the trial, Servetus acquitted himself well and with dignity.

The theological debate with Calvin was then resumed, conducted this time in writing so that there would be a written record to be shared with the other Swiss cities. The original thirty-eight charges were again levied, with Servetus responding by writing vitriolic comments directly on the manuscript that Calvin had supplied. In this exchange the two men were debating not so much the doctrine of the Trinity as the relationship between God and humanity. Servetus was convinced that Calvin's doctrines of predestination, original sin, and total depravity reduced men and women to mere objects like logs and stones; Calvin was convinced that Servetus's doctrine of human divinity reduced God to the level of human sinfulness. Their differences were unreconciliable.

The proceedings were then delayed while Calvin turned his attention to addressing a new Libertine threat to seize political control (the Council had even annulled Berthelier's excommunication) and while the written transcript of the trial was being circulated by messenger to the Councils of the other Swiss cities. Servetus once again petitioned the Council, complaining of both the delays and the miserable conditions in the prison: "The lice eat me alive. My clothes are torn and I have nothing for a change, neither jacket nor shirt, but a bad one." He also reminded the Council that his accuser had been released before the case had been decided, and he argued that both de la Fontaine and Calvin should be punished if their charges were not upheld. The Council's only response was that new clothes should be supplied Servetus, at his own expense.

A week later (it was by now September 22), Servetus sent yet another petition to the Council, requesting that Calvin should be imprisoned until the case was decided and listing six questions that he should be required to answer. All had to do with Calvin's communications to the Catholic court, with the final one asking, "Whether he did not well know that it is not the office of a minister of the gospel to make a capital accusation and to pursue a man at law to the death?" On October 10 he was to write again: "As for what you commanded that something be done to keep me clean, nothing has been done and I am in a worse state than before. . . . For the love of God, honored sirs, give your order whether for pity or duty." The Council again voted a change of clothing.

By the first of October a messenger had brought replies from Zürich, Bern, Basel, and Schaffhausen, where in each city the Council had referred the matter to the ministers to prepare the response. Their judgments were unanimous: Servetus was guilty of grave heresies—heresies that, if left unchecked, threatened to undermine the whole Reformation. The response of Zürich was typical of the rest: "We judge that one should work against him with great faith and diligence, especially as our churches have an ill repute abroad as heretics and patrons of heretics. God's holy providence has now indeed provided the occasion whereby you may at once purge yourselves and us from this fearful suspicion of evil." Just how this purging was to take place was left up to the Council at Geneva. The Council, aware of the importance of its decision, acted slowly and deliberately. A Libertine member urged that the case be transferred to a higher authority, the Council of 200. (The Council trying the case consisted of twenty-five members and was ordinarily referred to as the Little Council.) The ministers of the city argued that death by the sword, rather than by the stake, would be appropriate and more humane. Neither suggestion was followed. On October 27, 1553, a verdict was reached: Michael Servetus was found guilty of spreading heresies, particularly those relating to the Trinity, the eternal deity of Christ, and infant baptism, and was condemned "to be bound and taken to Champel and there attached to a stake and burned with [his] book to ashes." The sentence was to be carried out that very day.

Calvin later reported how Servetus, who had been hopeful of either exoneration or a much lighter sentence, reacted to the verdict: "At first he was stunned and then sighed so as to be heard throughout all of the room; then he moaned like a madman and had no more composure than a demoniac. At length his cries so increased that he continually beat his breast and bellowed in Spanish, '*Misericordia! misericordia!*'" Servetus's first request, after he regained his composure, was to meet with Calvin. When he asked for forgiveness, Calvin replied that he "had never entertained any personal rancor against him" and that, "if he would return to reason," he would do his best "to reconcile him to all good servants of God." Further, Calvin said that Servetus should "ask the pardon of God whom he had so basely blasphemed in his attempt to efface the three persons in the one essence" and should "beg the pardon of the Son of God" whom he had denied as being the "sole Redeemer." "But when I saw that all this did no good, I did not wish to be wiser than my Master allows. So following the rule of St. Paul, I withdrew from the heretic who was self-condemned."

Fearing that in his final agony at the stake he might recant his beliefs and thus lose his soul, Servetus had requested that he might die by the sword; the request was denied. It was

Guillaume Farel, not John Calvin, who accompanied him to Champel, a place outside the city gates. There he was bound by an iron chain to a stake surrounded by a pile of green wood. A crown of straw and leaves sprinkled with sulphur was placed on his head and his book tied to his arm. It was reported that when the executioner brought the torch before his face, he let out such a terrifying scream that the spectators shrank back in horror. As the fire burned around him he cried out, "O Jesus, Son of the eternal God, have pity on me!" In half an hour it was over. Farel pointed out that if Servetus had only shifted the position of the adjective and invoked the "eternal Son of God," his soul would have been saved. But Michael Servetus had placed the adjective where he believed it belonged—even in his final agony, he had not recanted.

The Double Legacy of Michael Servetus

The Scriptures are full of enigmas and inscrutable questions which have been in dispute for over a thousand years without agreement, nor can they be resolved without love, which appeases all controversies. Yet on account of these enigmas the earth is filled with innocent blood. . . . On controversial points we would do better to defer judgment, even as God, who knows us to be guilty, yet postpones judgment and waits for us to amend our lives.

To kill a man is not to defend a doctrine. It is simply to kill a man.

—SEBASTIAN CASTELLIO

*W*hy has the execution of Michael Servetus attracted such widespread attention down through the years? After all, thousands of other men and women were put to death as heretics or nonbelievers in those times, many of them in an equally cruel manner. There is a two-part answer to this question: first, his death was the catalyst that slowly led to the growth of religious tolerance; second, Servetus's writings led many to reconsider and revise some of the most basic doctrines of Christianity. Thus, when he died on the stake at Champel, Servetus left a double legacy to the world.

Reaction to the execution at first appeared to be favorable (Philip Melanchthon, now the chief spokesman for the Lutherans, and most of the leading Swiss Reformers had publicly expressed their approval); it was not long, however, before criticism began to surface. John Calvin responded by hurriedly putting into print a tract, *A Defense of the Orthodox*

Faith Against the Errors of Michael Servetus (Defensio Orthodoxae Fidei), published in February 1554, in which he attempted to defend the execution. Every chance had been given Servetus to escape death, Calvin claimed, but he had persisted in his shocking heresies and irreverent ways, leaving no alternative; it was necessary to silence this heretic to prevent souls from being lost. (How this related to the doctrine of predestination was not made clear.) Evidence of Calvin's great patience and Servetus's insulting language were reported in detail; nowhere did Calvin express any hint of remorse. "Seldom if ever in religious history," stated Earl Morse Wilbur, "has posthumous insult been more violent or odious, or more self-righteously used as in the service of God."

Hardly a month had passed after the publication of this tract when a book appeared in Basel, titled *Concerning Heretics, Whether They Are to be Persecuted (De Haereticis)*. The body of the book consisted of statements supporting religious tolerance taken from a broad spectrum of Christian writers. What was particularly galling to Calvin was the inclusion of a passage from his own writings. The most important part of the book, however, was a dedication to Duke Christoph of Württemberg (a duchy in southwest Germany) by "Martin Bellius." This essay argued that heresy is not an absolute, but a relative concept. "We are all heretics in the eyes of those who do not share our views," the author stated. ". . . Let us be tolerant towards one another, and let no one condemn another's belief." It included a rebuttal of the usual arguments for persecution and quite specifically condemned the treatment of Servetus.

> Who would wish to be a Christian, when he saw that those who confessed the name of Christ were destroyed by Christians themselves with fire, water, and the sword without mercy and more cruelly treated than brigands and murderers? Who would not think Christ a Moloch, or some such god, if he wished that men should be

immolated to him and burned alive? Who would wish to serve Christ on condition that a difference of opinion on a controversial point with those in authority should be punished by burning alive at the command of Christ himself more cruelly than in the bull of Phalaris, even though from the midst of the flames, he should call with a loud voice upon Christ, and should cry out that he believed in Him. Imagine Christ, the judge of all, present. Imagine Him pronouncing the sentence, and applying the torch. Who would not hold Christ for a Satan? What more could Satan do than burn those who call upon the name of Christ?

Calvin suspected, correctly, that "Martin Bellius" was none other than Sebastian Castellio, professor of Greek at the University of Basel; a man with such dangerous views must certainly be bridled.

Some enmity already existed between the two men. A dozen years earlier, Calvin had invited Castellio to come to Geneva to be rector of the college there, but when the latter sought to supplement his inadequate salary through appointment as one of the city's ministers, his application was rejected on theological grounds: he did not believe that the Song of Solomon was worthy of inclusion in the Bible nor did he accept the interpretation of Christ's descent into hell given in the Geneva Catechism (a summary of Calvinist doctrines). Castellio blamed Calvin for the rejection, and thenceforth the two became increasingly critical of each other. Bitter and resentful, Castellio moved to Basel, where, after living for several years in poverty, he received his professorial appointment.

Calvin and his followers had good reason to be concerned over the publication of *Concerning Heretics*, for it made a strong impression in the Swiss churches. Italian and French refugees who had fled to Switzerland to escape the Catholic Inquisition were fearful that a Protestant Inquisition might be in the process of emerging. Their concern was shared by

Humanists and Protestants who had remained in Italy and France. Given the strong reaction, Théodore Beza, Calvin's ministerial colleague at Lausanne and later his ecclesiastical successor at Geneva, realized that a response to Castellio was imperative. "If what he has spewed out in his preface is to be endured," he wrote a friend, "what, pray, have we left of the Christian religion? The doctrines of the office of Christ, the Trinity, the Lord's Supper, baptism, free will, the state of souls after death, are either useless or not necessary to salvation. No one is to be condemned as a heretic. You see what this leads to. I have therefore decided to reply."

In his reply, published that September, Beza began by denouncing Servetus as "of all the men that have ever lived the most wicked and blasphemous" and those that had condemned his death as "emissaries of Satan." He then went on to rebut Castellio point by point and to argue on scriptural and historical grounds that heretics are to be punished—in extreme cases, by death. Society's chief responsibility, he maintained, is to protect religion from corruption, and Castellio, by relativizing religion, was thereby undermining society. Beza's presentation was analytical and well-done (he had been a lawyer before becoming a minister and theologian) and, resting as it did on the premise that the Trinity was a basic doctrine of Christianity, was highly satisfying to those who shared that premise.

Castellio's *Concerning Heretics* had not been written as an answer to Calvin's *A Defense of the Orthodox Faith*; rather, the two had appeared almost simultaneously, prompted by sharply contrasting reactions to Servetus's death. But now that *A Defense* had appeared, Castellio decided to bypass Beza and attack Calvin directly. By year's end he had completed the manuscript of *Against Calvin's Book (Contra libellum Calvini)*. Castellio made it clear from the outset that he was writing neither to defend nor reject Servetus's opinions—in fact, he had never read his books—but rather to expose and condemn Calvin's actions and motives. He wrote:

Jehan Calvin enjoys great authority today, and I could wish he enjoyed even more did I know him to be of gentler disposition. But his last public action was a bloody execution followed by threats leveled at a number of pious persons. That is why I, who detests the shedding of blood (should not all the world do this?), have undertaken, with God's help, to disclose Calvin's purposes to the world, or at least to bring back into the right path some of those he has led astray.

On October 27, 1553, the Spaniard, Miguel Servetus, was burned in Geneva on account of his religious convictions, the instigator of the burning being Calvin, pastor of the cathedral in that city. This action has roused many protests, especially in Italy and France. In answer to these protests, Calvin has just issued a book, which seems to be most adroitly tinted. The author's aim is to justify himself, to attack Servetus, and to prove that Servetus was rightly punished by death. I propose to subject this book to a critical examination. In accordance with his usual controversial manner, Calvin will probably describe me as one of Servetus's disciples, but I hope that no one will thereby be misled. I am not defending the theses of Servetus, but am attacking the false theses of Calvin. I leave absolutely unconsidered discussions about baptism, the Trinity, and such matters. I do not even possess a copy of Servetus's books, since Calvin has burned all the copies he could lay his hands on; and I therefore do not know what ideas Servetus put forward. I shall do no more than pillory the errors of Calvin as to points which have no bearing upon differences of principle; and I hope to make clear to everyone what sort of man this is whom the lust for blood has driven crazy. I shall not deal with him as he dealt with Servetus, whom he committed to the flames, together with the books whose writing was deemed a crime—Servetus whom, even now when he is dead,

Calvin continues to revile. Calvin, having burned the
man and his books, has the audacity to refer us to these
books, quoting detached passages. It is as if an incendi-
ary, having reduced a house to ashes, were then to
invite us to inspect the furniture in the various rooms.
For my own part, I should never burn either an author
or his books. The book I am attacking is open to everyone, obtainable by everyone, in either of two editions,
one Latin and the other French. To avoid the possibility
of objection, I shall, in the case of every citation, put the
number of the paragraph from which it is taken, while
my answer to each passage will bear the same number
as the original.

The book then becomes a running commentary on Calvin's
volume in the form of a dialogue between Calvinus and
Vaticanus (Castellio), focused on the ethics of putting heretics
to death. Castellio's criticisms are biting, and often bitter and
sarcastic. For example:

If it is not blind rage to torture in the flames a man who
is calling on the name of Christ, and not only is not
convicted but is not even accused of any crime, then
there is no such thing as blind rage (page Cviii).
    To kill a man is not to protect a doctrine, but it is to
kill a man. When the Genevans killed Servetus, they did
not defend a doctrine, but they killed a man. To protest
a doctrine is not the Magistrate's affair (what has the
sword to do with doctrine?) but the teacher's. . . .
[W]hen Servetus fought with reasons and writings, he
should have been repulsed by reasons and writings
(page Eb).

Predictably, Calvin reacted with vehemence, if not blind
rage. Thereafter, from his power base in Geneva, he hounded
Castellio at every possible turn; the persecution would end

only with the death of the two men some nine years later. Publication of the book was blocked; for many years it circulated only in manuscript form. Fortunately, through all this travail, Castellio had the strong support of his students and colleagues at the university in Basel. It was said that, in that city, those guilty of profanity or lewd speech would be denounced as "Calvinists," a biting insult for that time and place.

The flurry of writings following Servetus's death (those of Calvin, Beza, and Castellio all appeared in little more than a year) did much to publicize Servetus's ideas; at least as importantly, it brought widespread attention to the matter of religious toleration. In Basel, northern Italy, England, Holland, and elsewhere, Castellio's ideas found receptive audiences. In Holland, especially, his writings were to play a major role as that country went through successive religious upheavals. It was there, as part of a struggle against the Dutch Calvinists by the Arminian Remonstrants (named after the Dutch theologian Jacobus Arminius, whose ideas the Remonstrants adopted), that *Against Calvin's Book* was finally published, some fifty years after it had been written. Earlier, Castellio's *Concerning Heretics*, as well as some of his other writings, had been reprinted.

Thus, part of the legacy of Michael Servetus, one that he could have neither planned nor foreseen, lies in the impetus that his death gave to the growth of religious toleration. As Earl Morse Wilbur has written,

> Emancipated souls who knew Servetus's doctrines, if at all, only as they were stated by his enemies and persecutors, and felt no sympathy for his heresies, yet totally disapproved of his being put to such a cruel death. His execution came to stand as a symbol of religious persecution at its worse, and his name as a symbol of martyrdom for freedom of conscience, even with those that knew or cared little for him as an individual. He thus . . . [had an] important influence in

stimulating the rise of religious toleration as a general policy, and the spread of tolerance of religious thought as an attitude of individual minds.

While heresy continued to be a capital crime in some Protestant countries well into the seventeenth century, the penalty had received what was to prove a mortal blow with the death of Michael Servetus.

The part of Servetus's legacy that he *did* plan lies in the impetus that his writings gave to the development of liberal Protestant thought. He wrote in an attempt to reform Christian theology before it could harden into dogma, and in this he was to a certain degree successful. Through his criticism of the traditional doctrine of the Trinity, he forced others to reconsider the doctrine for themselves, a reconsideration that was to lead to the rise of first, Socinianism, and then, Unitarianism. Servetus often has been claimed as a Unitarian martyr, but to make such a claim is to stretch the truth, for in a sense he was a trinitarian; it was only the traditional view of the natures of the Father, Son, and Holy Spirit, and the relationships between them, that he was attacking. Had he been blessed with a less obnoxious personality, and had his book *The Restoration of Christianity* not been so effectively suppressed, his influence doubtless would have been greater. While much of his influence was of a general nature, his writings did make a strong and direct impact, not only in Switzerland, but also in Italy, Poland, and Transylvania, and to a lesser extent in England and Germany.

The two books that Servetus published in 1531 and 1532, *On the Errors of the Trinity* and *Two Dialogues on the Trinity*, appear to have made just such a strong and direct impact on the Anabaptists of northern Italy, particularly in the region around Venice. In contrast to the Anabaptists living north of the Alps, who were mostly of the peasant class and had little interest in theology, those in Italy were more intellectual, with a genuine concern for doctrinal matters. As early as 1539 a letter signed by Philip Melanchthon was received by the Venetian Council. "I have learned," it read, "that a book of Servetus is being circulated there, which has revived the error of Paul of Samosata condemned by the primitive church. . . . I have thought that you should be warned and entreated to urge and encourage them to avoid, renounce, and detest the wicked error of Servetus."

Others, both Protestant and Catholic, also voiced their concern about the spread of Servetus's thought. "The Servetian plague is spreading," wrote one Protestant, and a papal bull (an official document from the pope) condemned as apostates those who denied the Trinity and the divinity of Christ. They had good reason to be concerned, for by mid-century, antitrinitarian Anabaptist groups had been organized in about sixty places in Italy and were ordaining ministers and bishops; the Venetian congregation alone had more than 1,000 members. At a council held in Venice, the approximately sixty delegates in attendance reached consensus after forty days on ten points of doctrine:

1. Christ is not God but man, born of Joseph and Mary, but filled with all the powers of God;
2. Mary had other sons and daughters after Christ;
3. There is no angelic being created by God, but where Scripture speaks of angels it means men appointed by God for a given purpose;
4. There is no other Devil but human prudence [i.e., cunning], for no creature of God is hostile to him but this;
5. The wicked do not rise at the last day, but only the elect, whose head is Christ;
6. There is no hell but the grave;
7. When the elect die, they sleep until the judgment day, when all will be raised;
8. The souls of the wicked perish with the body, as do all other animals;

9. The seed of man has from God the power of pro-
    ducing flesh and spirit;
10. The elect are justified by the eternal mercy and
    love of God without any outward work, that is,
    without the merits, the blood, or the death of Christ;
    Christ died to show forth the righteousness of
    God, that is, the sum of all the goodness and mercy
    of God and of his promises.

These ten points show a remarkable independence of thought,
integrating as they do portions of antitrinitarian, universalist,
Calvinist, and Lutheran theology; the tenth point bears a
striking resemblance to the doctrine of the atonement formulated some 250 years later by the American Universalist Hosea
Ballou.

The delegates of the Venetian council appointed two ministers to visit the various congregations, instructing them on
this body of doctrine, by far the most radical yet to appear in
the Protestant world. However, after a year on this mission,
one of the two ministers, a former priest, returned to the
Catholic Church and gave detailed depositions to its inquisitors about the congregations, their organization, and the names
and addresses of individual members. Arrests and prosecu-
tions soon followed, with the result that this remarkable
movement—which might have done much for the cause of
freedom, reason, and tolerance in religion—was quickly
destroyed. It was but a brief and tragic episode, with little, if
any, historical connection with things to come.

A more persisting influence of Servetus's thought, one that
has played a significant part in the evolution of the Unitarian
Universalist movement, comes principally by way of a number
of Italian Humanists who were Servetus's contemporaries and
who made their way to Switzerland to distance themselves
from the Catholic Inquisition. Given the great impact of the
Renaissance on Italy and the concurrent rise of Humanism
there, it is not surprising that many Italians undertook a

reexamination of traditional Christian doctrine. Whereas in such countries as Switzerland, Holland, Poland, and England this reexamination gave rise to reform, in Italy the Roman Catholic Church soon blocked such efforts. Most Italian Humanists either continued to accept the traditional Catholic doctrines or kept silent about their reservations, but a few felt compelled to seek an atmosphere of greater religious freedom. This they found in Swiss cities such as Geneva and Zürich, where, with Calvin's blessing, they established their own congregations. There, in their enthusiasm for reform, they openly debated doctrinal points, sometimes voicing heretical views in the process. As their discussions were held in Italian, Calvin was hampered in his usual efforts to monitor all religious proceedings. The trial and execution of Michael Servetus inevitably brought attention to the doctrine of the Trinity, and it was among these Italian expatriates that the seeds of Unitarianism were sown.

On the day following Servetus's execution, with the ashes at Champel still warm, there passed through Geneva an Italian expatriate, Bernardino Ochino, a former Franciscan friar who had left Catholicism to embrace the Reformation. Even though he professed Calvinist beliefs and had earlier served a congregation in Geneva, he was shocked by the news of what had happened to Servetus. His own experience had predisposed him toward toleration, for eleven years earlier he had been forced to flee from Italy because of his views. As a gaunt, roughly garbed, barefoot, and bareheaded ascetic, he had become the most renowned preacher in the whole of Italy. But as his preaching became progressively less traditional, influenced by his association with Humanist thinkers and by reading the works of those same Reformers he had been assigned to refute, he came under suspicion of heresy. Summoned to appear before the newly established Italian Inquisition, he was faced with the choice of either renouncing his views or being condemned to death. Instead, he decided to save both his conscience and his life by escaping to Switzerland in the late summer of 1542, one step ahead of the inquisitors. Safely there, he became an enthusiastic supporter of the Reformation, married, and earned a reputation as a competent pastor and scholar.

At the time of Servetus's death in 1553, Ochino was just returning from England, whither he had gone at the invitation of Archbishop Thomas Cranmer to support King Edward VI's efforts to promote the newly begun English Reformation. It had been a productive five years, during which he had published several volumes of sermons and a polemic against the papacy, which he dedicated to the young king. Princess Elizabeth (later to become Queen Elizabeth I, or "Good Queen Bess") read his sermons and even sought his spiritual advice; later, he was to dedicate a book to her. Doubtless Ochino would have stayed longer in England, but when Edward suddenly died in July 1553, Elizabeth's half-sister Mary ("Bloody Queen Mary"), a militant Catholic, inherited the throne and forced all foreign Protestants to leave the country. Cranmer himself was burned at the stake as a heretic.

Ochino did not tarry in Geneva; he found the atmosphere there too oppressive. After going first to the more liberal climate of Basel, where his friend Castellio resided, he settled in Zürich as pastor of a Protestant congregation of Italian exiles. There in 1563 he published two volumes of *Dialogues,* translated from Italian to Latin by Castellio. It presented various conflicting views with regard to Jesus, the Trinity, polygamy, and other topics. Théodore Beza, soon to succeed Calvin as the leader of the Reformation at Geneva, warned Heinrich Bullinger, leader of the Reformation in Zürich, that *Dialogues* favored the heresies of Servetus, but Bullinger did not at first take the charge seriously. No one raised significant objections until it was contended, in an impromptu discussion at an inn in Basel, that the book supported polygamy, a practice condoned by some of the Anabaptist and other radical Reformers.

The Council at Zürich investigated the matter and, with

the reputation of the city at stake, concluded that the *Dialogues* did indeed support the practice; subsequently it also found Ochino's views on the Trinity and other doctrines to be heretical. By then, Bullinger had turned against Ochino; he was removed from his pastorate and banished from the region. His plea to remain in Zürich through the winter with his four young children (by then he was seventy-six years old and a widower) was denied; in December he left the city with his family. Thereafter, branded as a heretic, Ochino went from pillar to post in search of a new home. In Nürnberg, Germany, where he found refuge until spring, he wrote his final book, defending himself against the charges that had been leveled against him and bitterly upbraiding Bullinger and the Council for their action.

Eventually the little family made its way to Kraków, in Poland, where it found a warm reception. Unfortunately, the Catholic authorities had been keeping track of Ochino's whereabouts and, having some influence in that city, forced the local magistrates to issue an edict of banishment. Ochino agreed to obey the edict, even though he feared he would die on the road or be eaten by wolves in the forest, but before he could leave, the whole family was smitten by the plague; only he and one daughter survived. Together they made their way to Moravia, where they found shelter in an Anabaptist colony. There Ochino soon died, condemned by Protestants and Catholics alike as both an Anabaptist and a Servetian.

Unlike Servetus, however, Ochino had never attacked the Trinity directly; his interest had been to keep the discussion of that and other doctrines alive. Before his death, he said, "I had much to endure, but this no apostle and disciple of Christ is spared. However, that I was enabled to endure all is proof that the Lord manifested his power in me." Bernardino Ochino's theological influence was to survive for a full century, both on the Continent and in England; but important though that influence may have been, he is best remembered as an examplar of the principles of free inquiry and religious tolerance.

In the summer of 1547, some six years after Ochino first had fled to Switzerland from Italy, another Italian, Laelius Socinus, crossed that same border. In many ways the two men were quite different—Socinus was far younger (only twenty-two at the time; Ochino had been fifty-five); came from an established, well-to-do Sienese family; and had studied for the law. But like Ochino, Socinus had become interested in the ideas of the Reformation and committed to its principles. Whether he left Italy out of fear of the Inquisition is uncertain; at any rate, he was eager to enter Switzerland and encounter the Reformation at first hand. Not lacking for funds, he first visited Geneva, where he had interviews with Calvin; then went on to Basel, where he likely met Castellio; thence to Navarre (an independent realm in the Pyrenees), where he visited the court of the Protestant queen; and finally to England, where he became acquainted with Ochino. Returning to Switzerland, by now well acquainted with Protestantism and some of its leaders, Socinus took up residency in Zürich; henceforth that city was to serve as his home base.

By all accounts, Socinus had the mind of a lawyer, skeptical and inquiring, but at the same time his warm, open personality and modest, undogmatic manner enabled him to make friends wherever he went. He evidently had a deep concern to formulate a sound, personal theology for himself, and as a result he was eager to question and converse with any of the Reformers who might provide him with insights. Thus he was in correspondence with Calvin, sought out Melanchthon in Wittenberg, and developed a close friendship with Bullinger, fostered in part by their living in the same city. (It would be a decade before Bullinger was to play a major role in banishing Ochino from the city; by then Socinus had died an early death.) The friendship became strained, however, by the death of Servetus; Bullinger supported Calvin's position, while Socinus openly disapproved of the execution.

In addition, Calvin, Beza, and others began to suspect that Socinus not only had collaborated with Castellio in the publication of *Concerning Heretics*, but harbored heretical views himself; certainly Servetus's execution had focused his attention on the Trinity, and he had continued in his persistent questioning on matters of faith. Bullinger, after interrogating Socinus as to his beliefs, was satisfied with his friend's doctrinal soundness but asked him to prepare a written profession of faith to lay the matter to rest. A critical examination of Socinus's resulting statement shows that he had left room for broad freedom of interpretation.

> I, Laelius Socinus, in my boyhood learned one creed, that which is called the Apostles' Creed, which I even now acknowledge to be the most ancient, accepted at all times in the Church, though drawn up in various forms. But I have read others also, and attribute all the honor I can and ought to the very old creeds of Nicaea and Constantinople.

Socinus, while never really committing himself to those ancient creeds in his statement, went on to acknowledge that the technical terms of the doctrine of the Trinity and Christology had been in use for 1,300 years, "from the time of Justin Martyr," whereas he would like to hear "the evangelical faith [expressed] in the words of Christ, the Apostles, and the Evangelists." He professed, among other things, to reject "the errors of Servetus and the whole Arian theology" (a theology based on the views of Arius, who held that Christ was a lesser being than God the Father) and those of the Anabaptists as well, without ever identifying any of them. Although Socinus's language appears evasive, this may well have been, not to dissimulate, but rather because of his innate cautiousness and his reluctance to express himself with certainty on speculative points of doctrine. At any rate, Bullinger was again satisfied with his friend's orthodoxy, and the two men shook hands in confirmation. Thereafter Socinus took pains to avoid further suspicion.

When in 1556 his father died, the Inquisition impounded his inheritance, leaving him with no means of support. Socinus determined to return to Italy in order to claim his patrimony, but in order to do so without being arrested it was necessary for him to go as a representative of a foreign power. Accordingly he visited Poland and Austria, receiving the necessary credentials from the rulers in both countries. His efforts proved to be in vain, however, for he found his family under persecution and the Inquisition unwilling to surrender any part of his father's estate.

Returning to Zürich, Socinus became more and more withdrawn from society as he worked to organize the results of his years of reading, inquiry, and thought. He died in 1562 at the age of thirty-seven. Had he lived a year longer, he doubtless would have interceded on behalf of Ochino when the latter came under attack; the two men had become friends, drawn together by their common interest in theology and their commitment to free inquiry.

Little that Socinus wrote ever appeared in print; hence it is impossible to know the details of his evolving system. It is apparent, however, that as he worked to build that system, he came to give reason a weight equal to that of scripture; in this he was a true pioneer. One of his most significant contributions was a radical reinterpretation of John 1 in which the phrase "the beginning" referred not to the time of creation, but rather to the time when Jesus began to preach; he thus moved the scene of action from the cosmic to the historical plane, rejected the preexistence of Christ, and gave Christology a humanistic thrust. At his death his nephew Faustus came at once to take possession of his uncle's library and manuscripts. The latter were to play a major role in the development of Faustus's own thought and hence of the Socinian movement in Poland, a precursor to Unitarianism. Thus Laelius Socinus can aptly be called the patriarch of Polish Socinianism.

Among the other Italian Humanists who migrated northward and subsequently helped sow the seeds of Unitarianism, four are especially worthy of mention: Matteo Gribaldi, a professor of law; Gianpaolo Alciati, a nobleman; Giovanni Gentile, a teacher of Latin; and Giorgio Biandrata, a physician. All except Gentile were from northern Italy; indeed, most of the antitrinitarian reformers were from Piedmont, Lombardy, Veneto, or the Grisons, now the Swiss canton of Graubunden. Gentile, from Calabria, in the "toe" of Italy, was a rare exception.

Matteo Gribaldi, a native of Chieri, near Turin, was passing through Geneva at the time of Servetus's trial on his way from his summer home near Geneva to Padua, where he taught at the university. Learning of the case, he not only stated that he opposed the death penalty for heresy, but also that he agreed with Servetus's views; in fact, until reading *On the Errors of the Trinity*, he never really had known Christ. Only a few months after the execution, an *Apology for Michael Servetus* appeared, written under a pseudonym, but apparently Gribaldi's work. For the rest of his life, as he attempted to pursue an academic career in Germany and France, Gribaldi was under almost constant surveillance by the Calvinists and intermittently questioned as to his beliefs. Eventually he was charged with heresy and imprisoned—he had under duress accepted the Apostles' and Nicene Creeds but not the Athanasian.

To escape martyrdom and obtain his release, Gribaldi finally signed a confession renouncing his heretical statements and subscribing to the Athanasian Creed. Once an immensely popular professor, he died of the plague in 1564, already widowed and deserted by his children and friends. At best only an amateur theologian, he had concluded that Father, Son, and Holy Spirit were three distinct beings, each of them fully God, with the Father the source of the other two; only in an abstract sense were the three a unity, manifesting one power and wisdom. Gribaldi's tritheism had but limited and brief support, but it did serve as a bridge between Servetus and the Socinianism that was soon to emerge in Poland.

Gianpaolo Alciati, a native of the Piedmont, had followed a military career until the middle of the century, when, still in his thirties, he moved to Geneva and became a member of the

Protestant congregation of Italian exiles; there he became a friend of both Gentile and Biandrata. During the controversy following Servetus's execution, Alciati, who had risen to the position of elder, shocked many of his fellow parishioners by taking a strong antitrinitarian position. "We worship three devils," he said, "worse than all the idols of the Papacy, because we make it three persons." It was a time of great intolerance in Geneva; Alciati was declared an enemy of the church and his property seized. An Italian visitor to the city, Caterina Coppa, shocked at what she found going on there, was reported to have said that Alciati and Gentile held good doctrine and had been wrongly persecuted; she was tried, found guilty, and forced to make a retraction in order to escape beheading. Alciati stoutly defended his views in writing, at the same time attacking Calvin's oppressive leadership. After being banished forever from Geneva on pain of death, he set out for Poland, where he helped lay the foundation for the Socinian movement.

Giorgio Biandrata arrived in Geneva in 1556, having escaped from Lombardy after the Inquisition became suspicious of his views. He was forty years old at the time and had previously practiced medicine both in Italy and in Poland; in the latter country he had served for some dozen years as the personal physician of both the Polish queen and her daughter, wife of the king of Hungary. Once in Geneva he joined the Italian congregation and made the acquaintance of Gribaldi and Alciati; like the latter he became one of the church's elders. It was not long before he began to raise doctrinal questions, often directed at Calvin, and to search for clearer definitions of theological terms. At first Calvin responded with patience, but gradually, as so often happened, he became annoyed and termed Biandrata a troublemaker.

In 1558 the members of the Italian congregation were called together and asked to subscribe to a confession of faith drawn up to counteract the heretical views that had begun to surface concerning the Trinity and the nature of Christ. Calvin invited those present to express their views openly, assuring them that nothing they said would be held against them. After a heated discussion Biandrata joined Alciati in refusing to sign the confession (Gribaldi was not then in Geneva). He, too, was banished from the city and made his way to Poland. "Warn the good brethren," wrote Calvin to a Polish friend, "before they learn by experience what a monster Giorgio Biandrata is, or rather, how many monsters he fosters, to beware of him." Despite Calvin, Giorgio Biandrata was to play an important part in the Socinian/Unitarian movement, not only in Poland but in Transylvania as well.

One of those who *did* subscribe to the aforementioned confession of faith was Giovanni Gentile, who two years earlier had made his way northward to Geneva to join the Italian congregation there. Subsequently, with Gribaldi, Alciati, and Biandrata gone, it appeared that the church might experience a period of doctrinal harmony, but its pastor persisted in keeping controversy alive by continually attacking some of the signers of the confession as really being Arians and Servetians. Gentile, who had delayed in signing and had done so only with some reluctance, was reported by one of Calvin's undercover spies as having privately expressed heretical views; he was arrested and questioned at length.

Then, in a written statement of beliefs ordered by the Council, Gentile was incautious enough to disagree with Calvin's understanding of the Godhead, claiming that the latter had described, not a Trinity, but a Quaternity. After Calvin reacted angrily, Gentile attempted to ameliorate the situation by retracting some of his statements, only to be found guilty of both heresy and perjury. He was condemned to be beheaded, but after members of the Italian community interceded on his behalf, the sentence was commuted to one of public recantation and humiliation. Dressed only in a shirt and carrying a lighted torch in his hand, he was led through the city streets to the blast of trumpets, having first confessed his heresies and burned his writings.

Retreating to the safety of Lyons, Gentile then wrote a long manuscript entitled *Antidota* in which he again attacked Calvin's doctrine of the Trinity and presented one of his own; it resembled, and was doubtless influenced by, the tritheism of Gribaldi. Thereafter he was widely condemned for his views, not only in Switzerland, but also in France and Poland, a country that he visited to support the emerging antitrinitarian movement there. In the end he was tried in Bern, charged with seven specific errors concerning the Trinity, with making false accusations against church leaders, and with practicing deception to avoid punishment. Found guilty and condemned to die by the sword, he was given the opportunity to save his life by subscribing to the same confession that Gribaldi had signed nine years earlier. This time Gentile remained true to his convictions and refused to recant; he approached the block denouncing the clergy present as Sabellians—the heresy claiming that God existed in three "modes"—and declaring that he was dying as a martyr in the name of the one true God.

When Giovanni Gentile was executed in 1566, thirteen years after Michael Servetus, no voices were raised in protest. Castellio was dead, and no one had yet dared to take his place; Calvin and Beza had managed to suppress dissent in Protestant Switzerland as effectively as the Inquisition had in Catholic Italy. It would not be long, however, before new voices would champion the cause of toleration. As for Servetus's ideas, they were to survive through his writings. Though outdated within a few generations, they had provided the crucial catalyst that would initiate the Unitarian movement. Thus his legacy was truly twofold.

Faustus Socinus
and the Rise of Polish Socinianism

*Q. What are the things that concern his [Christ's]
Essence or Person?*

*A. Only that he is a true man by nature, as the holy
Scriptures frequently testifie concerning that matter, and namely, 1 Tim. 2.5. . . .*

Q. Hath he not also a divine Nature?

*A. At no hand; for that is repugnant not only to sound
Reason, but also to the holy Scriptures.*

—THE RACOVIAN CATECHISM

*S*ocinians traditionally marked the beginning of their movement with an incident that took place in the Polish capital of
Kraków in 1546. At that time a group of distinguished Catholic Humanists was meeting regularly in private homes to discuss theological matters and possible ways in which to reform
the Catholic Church. At one such meeting a non-Catholic
guest from Holland was present, later identified only as "Spiritus." While the group was waiting for dinner, he glanced
through a book of prayers he had taken from the shelf. Some
of the prayers, he found, were addressed to God the Father,
others to God the Son, and yet others to God the Holy Spirit.
"What," he asked, "have you here three gods?" Being told by
the others that they had one god in three persons, he pursued
the matter, and a lively discussion ensued. Spiritus's question
was not forgotten; in the minds of some of those present it
stuck like a barb. Among those most affected was Francesco
Lismanino, a prominent leader of the Catholic Church; he
would soon leave Catholicism to help lead the liberal,

antitrinitarian wing of the Polish Reformation out of which Socinianism was to emerge.

Ten years later, in January 1556, a Lithuanian named Peter Gonesius stood before a joint assembly (or synod) of Polish Calvinists and Bohemian Brethren, another Protestant group, in the city of Secemin, seeking admission to its membership. In doing so, he stated his beliefs, recorded as follows by the clerk:

1. He declared that the Trinity did not exist, and that the word was a new invention.
2. He criticized the Athanasian Credo, and rejected it completely as a "human invention."
3. God the Father is the sole God, and there is no other.
4. Christ is inferior to his Father, he is his father's servant.
5. He stated that *Logos* was The Word, invisible, immortal, transformed at a given time into flesh in the Virgin's womb, and he called this Word the seed of the Incarnated Son.
6. He denied the coexistence of Jesus Christ and God the Father within divinity.

All this Gonesius supported with quotations from scripture and from Irenaeus, one of the early Church Fathers. As a young man he had gone to Italy to study and lecture at the university in Padua. There it is probable that he met Matteo Gribaldi and became acquainted with his religious ideas. At any rate, while in Padua, Gonesius came under the influence of Servetian and Anabaptist thought. He returned to Poland a changed person, full of new religious and social views and wearing a wooden sword rather than a steel one in order to symbolize his pacifism. He was not, however, a flamboyant man; by all accounts he was dignified in manner and temperate and reasonable in debate. His statement to the synod had not been made to shock, but rather to express his carefully thought-through beliefs.

Gonesius's statement was by no means the first reported instance of antitrinitarianism in Poland. Several decades earlier, Katharine Weigel, at the age of seventy, had been accused by the Catholic Church of apostasy to Judaism. The charge had been dropped after she recanted, but ten years later she was accused again. This time Weigel did not recant; she freely confessed her faith in God, but she refused to say that she believed in Christ as his Son. Convicted of blasphemy, she was burned at the stake on April 19, 1539, in the market place at Kraków. It was reported that the white-haired eighty-year-old woman went to her death boldly and cheerfully, unwilling to compromise her beliefs.

The synod at Secemin, which had been so upset by Gonesius's views, was, however, unable to successfully refute his arguments. Finally in frustration it instructed him to consult with the Lutheran leader Philip Melanchthon at Wittenberg in the hope that Melanchthon would be able to convince him of his errors. Prayers were offered in his behalf and a collection taken to defray the cost of the journey; he left the meeting in tears. The trip proved futile, however, for Melanchthon, quickly concluding that Gonesius had been infected by antitrinitarian heresy, would have nothing further to do with him.

Rejected, Gonesius proceeded to publish a small volume outlining his views, particularly with respect to the divinity of Christ; it created an instant sensation. Never shy or easily discouraged, he then appeared at another joint synod where, by a nearly unanimous vote, he was excluded as an Arian. Finding himself no longer welcome in Poland, Gonesius returned to his native Lithuania, where his views helped initiate a flourishing antitrinitarian movement. With the support of some influential members of the nobility he was made pastor of the liberal Reformed congregation in the city of Wegrow, where he continued to live until his death in 1573 at the age of about fifty.

Meanwhile, Giorgio Biandrata, Gianpaolo Alciati, and Giovanni Gentile had visited Poland and helped to nurture the seeds that Gonesius had already sown; in fact, of the sixteen ministers who had attended the synod at Secemin, seven later became antitrinitarians, as did several of the laypeople present. By his later years most of the antitrinitarians in Poland and Lithuania had gone beyond Gonesius to a more radical theological position, but it was he who had given the movement its initial impetus, together with an ongoing commitment to social change.

The political, social, and religious situation in Poland was extremely complex during these times, but the combination of broadly dispersed political power, a tripartite Protestantism, and a relatively permissive Catholicism resulted in a climate favorable to the propagation of unorthodox religious views. The Reformed Church of Poland, Calvinist in its theology, had been organized in the 1550s, and the Lutherans and Bohemian Brethren, followers of the Czech priest Jan Hus who had been burned at the stake in 1415, both had localized strength.

Ironically, it was in the Reformed Church that the Socinian movement had its beginnings. For nearly a decade there had been a growing schism in that body over the doctrine of the Trinity. Biandrata and Laelius Socinus had arrived in 1558, Alciata and Gentile a few years later. By then the doctrine of the Trinity was being openly debated, with many ministers and laypeople coming to an antitrinitarian position. Calvin, when hearing of this development, brought all his power to bear to turn the tide. Synod meetings became increasingly fractious as those attending aligned themselves into two rival camps.

At the height of the controversy lightning struck the top of the steeple of Trinity Catholic Church in Kraków. The event caused a sensation; it was hailed by the antitrinitarians as a sign that God was on their side. The account was elaborated in the retelling; the lightning bolt was said to have struck at exactly high noon on Trinity Sunday (a special Sunday in the church year), in 1562, while a leading antitrinitarian minister,

Gregory Paulus, was preaching against the doctrine elsewhere in the city. Later it was claimed that lightning also struck the Trinity Church in another city on Trinity Sunday, just as it was being dedicated, and burned it to the ground! By 1565 the split was complete, with the orthodox Calvinists refusing any further association with those who had become antitrinitarian in their Christology. On June 10 of that year a synod was held at Brzeziny, the first such assembly attended exclusively by antitrinitarian congregations; it thus can be considered as marking historically the beginning of Unitarianism as an organized movement.

At first the new body resulting from the schism between the antitrinitarian and the orthodox Calvinists had no name, its members identifying themselves simply as "the brethren in Poland and Lithuania who have rejected the Trinity"; later the Minor Reform Church of Poland was adopted as its official title. (Despite the implications of its name, this new body was effectively stronger than the one from which it had separated.) Opponents of the Minor Church, whether Protestant or Catholic, referred to its members as "Arians." They themselves preferred to be called simply Christians or, later, the Polish Brethren; the terms Socinians and Socinianism were not devised until the next century and even then were adopted only abroad.

Two issues faced the new church: baptism and Christology. The Reformed Church of Poland, being Calvinistic, had of course advocated infant baptism, but Gonesius and others, influenced by Anabaptism, had rejected the practice as unscriptural and without efficacy. By the time the schism was complete, the issue had already been debated with increasing intensity for seven years, and by then many members of the Minor Church had already become supporters of adult baptism by immersion. The new church lost no time in facing up to the matter, beginning with meetings on Christmas Day, 1565. Debate was long and often heated, with the opponents of infant baptism holding the majority position. After six days, however, they agreed that "since in matters of faith no one in the true church of God may lord it over another, nor be forced, each should enjoy freedom of conscience and be allowed to publish writings on the subject, provided nothing was said or written calculated to anger another or openly contrary to Christ's command. Thus [says the chronicler] they kept love inviolate by stipulating only that no one should do anything against the honor of God or burdening to conscience." And so, from its beginning, the Minor Reformed Church affirmed the principle of mutual toleration both for itself and for the larger movement to which it helped give rise.

The matter of Christology was not so easily dealt with. The Italians Gribaldi, Gentile, and Alciati had, during their visits, promoted the idea that Father, Son, and Holy Spirit were three separate, preexistent beings, only one in the sense of having the same nature. This virtual tritheism was unacceptable to many antitrinitarians, and they soon abandoned it as they came to regard the Holy Spirit simply as the power of God at work in human life. Two competing views then emerged regarding the nature of the Son. Some, including Peter Gonesius, continued to ascribe preexistence and a measure of deity to Christ, though holding him subordinate to the Father; they became known as ditheists. Others denied any preexistence or deity to Jesus, regarding him as being fully human only; they had thus adopted a unitarian position.

The inevitable clash between the ditheists and unitarians took place at a synod held in the spring of 1567, with the debate becoming so angry that the meeting was adjourned for several weeks to allow tempers to cool. When it was reconvened, the numbers in attendance had swelled; over a hundred ministers and nobles from all parts of Poland and Lithuania were present, plus many residents of the immediate vicinity. Order and civility were maintained, and the discussion continued for five days. Although those in attendance could reach no agreement, they unanimously adopted a statement affirming mutual tolerance and the rights of conscience in belief and practice, with "no one wishing to impose his faith upon another, since this is the gift of God; and until he sends his angels to separate the tares from the wheat they are not to exclude or wound one another." Gradually, however, the unitarian position became predominant as the ditheists either abandoned their views or left the church.

In the meantime, Polish Catholicism was beginning to respond to the Reformation challenge with a newfound vitality. As a consequence, in 1570 the Calvinists, Lutherans, and Bohemian Brethren, in order to present a united Protestant front, formed a federation from which they deliberately excluded the Minor Church. Thereafter the antitrinitarians, who had sought inclusion, were forced to make their way alone, condemned by Catholics and Protestants alike as being outside the pale.

Fortunately, at this same time, a development occurred that was to have a profound and positive effect on the antitrinitarian movement. The wife of a wealthy Calvinist, Jadwige Gnoinskiej, herself an ardent "Arian," had become concerned about the plight of her fellow religionists, many of whom were suffering persecution. Determined to address the problem, she persuaded her husband to establish a new town where religious toleration would be guaranteed. Pleasantly situated in the country about seventy miles north of Kraków, the town was named Raków, for the *rak* or crab on the benefactress's coat of arms. Antitrinitarians and Anabaptists, including members of the nobility and ministers, were at once attracted to this "New Jerusalem," and the town grew rapidly.

Initially, chaos reigned, as property was held in common and people disowned all rank and ordinations. During 1570 horror stories about what was taking place in Raków abounded, and parallels to the debacle of the Anabaptist revolt at Münster were being drawn. The Polish Calvinists reported to their Swiss counterparts that many in the town had "reached such a pitch of madness that they deny not only the immortality of the soul, but even that there is in man any distinct soul whatsoever. . . . They are founding a town . . . in which all those of this sort are settling in order that they may perish there together. The very scum are joining this sect, a few of the gentry, none of the magnates as far as I know." After three years of continuous experimentation and with the whole venture on the verge of collapse, the needed leadership arose in the person of Simon Ronemberg, the town apothecary. Community of goods was abandoned, artisans and tradesmen established themselves, the ordained ministry was reinstituted and a church established. Thus reorganized, Raków was soon to become the strong center of the Socinian movement. Four decades after the town's founding a British visitor reported that

> when he had taken pains to pass through Raków, a town in Little Poland, where the heresy of the Socinians flourishes greatly, he felt as though he had been trans-ported into another world; for whereas elsewhere all was full of wars and tumult, there all was quiet, men were calm and modest in behavior, so that you might think them angels, although they were spirited in de-bate and expert in language.

The restoration of order in Raków under Ronemberg did not mean the end to social radicalism there and elsewhere among the "Arians," as others called them. Committed as they were to living by the teachings of Christ and the example of the early Christians, expressions of such radicalism were in-evitable, even though carried out in a more orderly fashion. The pacifist and socialist views of the Anabaptists were widely debated and embraced by many; several nobleman sold their estates, distributed the proceeds among the poor, and became common laborers.

There was doctrinal radicalism as well. Simon Budny, a Lithuanian minister and scholar, was condemned as a "Judaizer" and excommunicated from the Minor Reformed Church for contending that prayers should never be addressed to Christ—a rare example of antitrinitarian intolerance. (Judaism was attracting some converts, Katharine Weigel among them, and the willingness to address Christ in prayer had become the crucial test of one's Christian faith.)

On the whole, however, there continued to be broad tolerance for diverse doctrinal views within the Minor Church; indeed, the church found the social and political climate in Poland and Lithuania favorable. After the death of the king in 1572 (the two countries had united in 1569 to form a single kingdom), the Senate and Chamber of Deputies drew up an agreement known as the Confederation of Warsaw. It contained a provision for religious liberty that had been drafted jointly by Protestant and Catholic clergy:

> Since there is in our Republic no little disagreement on the subject of religion, in order to prevent any such hurtful strife from beginning among our people on this account as we plainly see in other realms, we mutually promise for ourselves and our successors forever, under the bond of our oath, faith, honor, and conscience, that we who differ with regard to religion will keep the peace with one another, and will not for a different faith or a change of churches shed blood nor punish one another by confiscation of property, infamy, imprisonment, or banishment, and will not in any way assist any magistrate or officer in such an act.

Polish Protestants had pressed hard for such a provision, especially since the Massacre of St. Bartholomew, in which some 50,000 French Protestants had been killed, had just taken place. The Confederation of Warsaw was to protect the antitrinitarians through the rest of the sixteenth century.

It was in 1579 that Faustus Socinus, nephew of Laelius, passed through Poland on his way to Transylvania, visiting some of his uncle's acquaintances on the way. His mission in Transylvania complete (he had attempted to mediate a doctrinal dispute among the antitrinitarians there), he returned to

Poland, found the religious climate congenial, and decided to settle there. The Minor Church at that time was in a state of disarray, with neither leadership nor doctrinal agreement. Perhaps forty congregations existed of varying sizes, composition, and emphases. Some were little more than chaplaincies on the estates of nobles; a few were sizable congregations in the larger towns and cities. Those in the southern part of Poland were conservative in theology but radical in social views; those to the northeast, in Lithuania, were radical in theology but conservative in social outlook. Membership, drawn from all strata of society, varied widely.

These disparate congregations were united on little more than a common rejection of the Trinity and an affirmation of the Bible as the only basis for conduct and belief; there was, however, little agreement as to what that conduct and belief should be. The holding of government office, the bearing of arms, capital punishment, the sharing of goods, the accumulation of wealth, the mode of baptism, the meaning of the Lord's Supper, the worship of Christ, the nature of the Holy Spirit, the coming of the millenium—on matters like these there was little accord. The fledgling church, now twenty years old, seemed on the point of disintegration. The appearance of a new leader in the person of Faustus Socinus was indeed timely, if not providential.

A member of a distinguished Sienese family, Faustus Socinus as a young man had found little focus to his life. A disinterested student, he failed to earn a degree; later, he spent twelve years as a Florentine courtier—years that he later considered as wasted. In 1574, at the age of thirty-five, he left Italy forever, settling for four years in Basel. Some years earlier, during a sojourn in Lyons, he had acquired the books and papers of his uncle Laelius. As he studied these his views began to be shaped and his interests to be centered on biblical interpretation and theology. He had already written, while still in Florence, a treatise upholding the authority of the Bible, *Concerning the Authority of the Sacred Scriptures (De*

Sacrae Scripturae Auctoritate), which had been widely acclaimed by Catholics and Protestants alike. Basel, he thought, would be the ideal place in which to cultivate his new interests, and, once there, he began to study and to write with renewed purpose.

It was while in Basel that Socinus wrote his most important theological work, *Concerning the Savior Jesus Christ (De Jesu Christo Servatore)*, in which he argued that Christ is Savior, not because of his death on the cross, but because his life showed men and women the way to salvation, which they can attain by following his example. Predictably, his thesis created controversy; it also brought him to the attention of Giorgio Biandrata, who had gone from Poland to Transylvania, there to aid the cause of reform. A dispute had arisen in that country over the propriety of addressing prayer to Christ, and Biandrata had summoned Socinus, as a promising young theologian, to help settle the matter. When, after a stay of several months, Socinus left Transylvania, he decided against returning to Basel where he might well have been charged with heresy; by contrast, Poland offered freedom of religious thought. Accordingly, he chose to settle in Kraków; Poland would be his home for the rest of his life.

Socinus almost immediately sought admission to membership in the Minor Church. Presenting himself to the synod meeting at Raków in 1580, he openly expressed his opposition to adult baptism as a condition for membership; for this there was, he maintained, no scriptural basis. The synod, however, insisted on baptism as a requirement. Socinus finally agreed to the rite on the condition that he first could state publicly that he believed it unnecessary and was participating simply for the sake of closer fellowship. His proposal was rejected, and repeated attempts to persuade him to change his mind all failed. As a consequence Socinus was never admitted to the celebration of the Lord's Supper nor to membership in the church he was destined to lead. "Was ever," commented Earl Morse Wilbur, "another such case in all Christian history?"

Although Socinus felt his exclusion keenly, he showed no resentment, nor, as is evident from subsequent events, did the members of the Minor Church turn their back on him or exclude him from their circle of trust. His participation in doctrinal discussions at synod meetings was welcomed and his reputation as an outstanding theologian soon recognized. Ministers sought his advice on a wide range of concerns, and he was soon involved in a voluminous correspondence with both supporters and critics.

Socinus wrote and circulated many tracts (anonymously at first) defending the Minor Church against outside attacks and welcoming opportunities to take its part in public debate. In addition, he addressed forthrightly a number of issues on which the antitrinitarians were divided. Specifically, he defended the practice of invoking Christ in prayer (not to do so would be a reversion to Judaism or to atheism), argued against any expectation of a millenial reign of Christ on earth (such a view had no scriptural support), and contended that the church must be pacifist (although a Christian should support the civil government unless it acted contrary to Christ's teachings). Some of the more radical Racovians found his opinions too moderate, but his wisdom and open and benign manner won him wide respect throughout the church.

During this same period the Catholic religious order of Jesuits established a center in Kraków from which they began mounting an ongoing assault on the Minor Church. Socinus's published works, though written anonymously, were being singled out as seditious, and even the king's suspicions had been aroused. As a consequence, Socinus was persuaded to move from Kraków to the nearby estate of a sympathetic nobleman where, under Polish law, he would be safe from danger. In this haven he stayed from 1583 until 1587, leading a quiet life, but extremely busy with his correspondence and writing. While there he married his host's daughter; soon afterward, the king having died, he moved back to Kraków with his bride. A daughter was born to the couple, but Socinus's joy was short-lived, for his wife Elizabeth died a few months later. He was overcome with grief and his health shattered, never to be fully regained. In addition, the income that he had been receiving from inherited properties in Italy was cut off; thereafter he had to rely on the generosity of friends. Socinus was, however, able to resume public life and to take part once more in synod deliberations to the extent his health permitted.

Meanwhile the hostility of the Catholics toward the members of the Minor Church continued to rise; in fact, in 1591 both the Calvinist and "Arian" churches in Kraków had been destroyed by angry mobs. Then, a leading Jesuit scholar published a tract on the divinity of Christ and the Holy Spirit and taunted the "Arians" for not making a reply. Socinus, by then the acknowledged spokesperson for his church, accepted the challenge, writing a powerful refutation that was published anonymously in the name of the church. Not long after the work appeared, Socinus, whom the Catholics had suspected of authorship, was attacked on the streets of Kraków by a group of carousing soldiers under the command of a Catholic noble. Filth was spread over his face and into his mouth, and he was forced to kneel as a suppliant at the drunken commander's feet. The commander later apologized, but the outrage was never punished.

A much more serious assault took place a few years later when a mob of students, celebrating Ascension Day (a special day in the Catholic church calendar), broke into the house where Socinus lay sick in bed, dragged him to the marketplace, burned the books and papers they had found in his room, and threatened to burn him as well if he did not recant. His reply was firm: "I do not recant, but what I have been I am and will be, by the grace of the Lord Jesus Christ, as long as I live; and you may do whatever God permits you." Taken aback, the students abandoned the idea of burning Socinus and decided to take him to the river and drown him instead; but as they passed the university, a professor, who had heard the noise, came out and persuaded the mob to turn the heretic over to him. Learning the bedraggled man's identity, he treated Socinus after the example of the Good Samaritan, clothing him in disguise and smuggling him to a safer place.

Later, after narrowly avoiding yet another attack, broken up by a violent thunder and hailstorm, Socinus managed to escape from the city at dawn, finding refuge at the estate of an Italian friend some fifteen miles away. His friend urged him to stay, but Socinus felt the need to settle in a place where the books he needed for his work were available and where he would be at safer distance from Kraków. Accordingly, as soon as he had sufficiently recovered, he moved to the village of Luclawice, some forty-five miles southeast of the capital; there he was to spend the remaining six years of his life, doing as much work as his health and failing eyesight permitted. His last important book, written at the request of a Calvinist friend, was a critique of the Polish Calvinist church. In it, Socinus charged that its reforms had been inadequate and its moral standards lax, and he urged all those who hungered for a genuine biblical faith and a disciplined Christian life to join the Minor Church. This small book evidently made a deep impression and inspired much discussion for a whole generation.

Concerned about the future of his church and realizing that his health was failing, Socinus in 1601 convened at Raków a meeting of a dozen leading ministers to discuss doctrinal matters. The meeting lasted for three whole weeks, with Socinus giving his own views in turn on such subjects as God, Christ, the Holy Spirit, humanity, sin, free will, the Bible, and the sacraments. Open discussion would follow, in which the attendees sought consensus on essentials and allowed for latitude on nonessentials. The discussions then turned from theology to such social issues as engaging in lawsuits, resisting physical force, and taking part in war. The format proved successful, with those present, including Socinus, modifying and refining their views through the verbal interchange.

The meeting was so productive that a second one was held the following year, attended by over twenty ministers and an equal number of lay leaders. On this occasion the proceedings were enlivened by spirited debates on the questions of oaths, capital punishment, the holding of private property, the charging of interest, the accumulation of wealth, and participation in war. As a result, some tempering of the more radical social views took place, largely through Socinus's influence. No consensus could be reached on the matter of war; although pacifism was strongly supported, those who believed war was permitted by scripture were not condemned. The two meetings had a unifying effect on the Minor Church as a whole; thereafter it was able to act with more accord on both doctrinal and social issues.

Faustus Socinus spent the last few years of his life collecting and editing his writings and working with some of the younger ministers on a catechism designed to give a clear exposition of the doctrines of the Minor Church. He died on March 3, 1604, at the age of sixty-four. His grave, in the "Arian" cemetery at Luclawice, is marked with an impressive monument erected in 1933 with funds donated by American Unitarians.

Much of Socinus's writings never appeared in print during his lifetime because of lack of funds. After his death, however, the Minor Church, determined to preserve his legacy, collected his writings, publishing those that had appeared only in manuscript and reprinting those that had been previously published. For the next quarter of a century, a steady flow of his books emanated from the church's press at Raków, some of them in German and Dutch translation. Thus was his thought disseminated throughout central and western Europe and, eventually, the world. The work on the catechism that Socinus and his followers had been writing was resumed. The first Polish edition was published in 1605, the second in 1619; it is generally known as the *Racovian Catechism*, after its place of publication (its official title is over fifty words long!).

Despite its name, the book is not a catechism in the usual sense, that is, a book of instruction for the young; rather, it is a summary of doctrine, in question-and-answer form, prepared for purposes of propaganda and defense. German, Dutch, and Latin editions soon appeared, evoking scathing criticism from trinitarian presses in Poland and Germany. The translator of the Latin edition presumed to dedicate his volume to James I of England, a monarch noted for his support of Protestantism; but when the king examined its contents, he denounced it as satanic, and it was burned by order of Parliament. Thus well publicized, the *Racovian Catechism* was widely read and became a source of continuing vexation to both Calvinists and Lutherans.

The catechism, while composed in its final form by others, clearly reflects Socinus's teachings. It is based squarely on scripture, and its central theme is the achievement of eternal life through the knowledge of God and Christ and the following of God's will as revealed by Christ. Thus the emphasis is on disciplined human conduct. Predestination is specifically repudiated; men and women have free will to seek their own salvation. Also repudiated are original sin and the orthodox doctrine of atonement, which teaches that Christ died on the cross to atone for the sins of humanity; it asserted instead that Christ suffered on the cross to demonstrate how suffering should be endured. It of course rejected the doctrine of the Trinity: God is only one person, not three; Christ is a true man without a divine nature, although uniquely God's Son. As such, he is to be adored—indeed, the invocation of Christ is the mark of the true Christian. The Holy Spirit is not a person in the Godhead, but a divine power at work in human hearts. Thus the catechism is not only antitrinitarian in its theology, it is also unitarian.

The catechism presented the Ten Commandments and Christ's teachings as a guide to personal and social behavior, and it strongly emphasized that secular and civil relations are subject to the will of God—a Christian must obey the laws of the state provided they do not violate the laws of God; under this same condition a Christian may hold public office and bring suit in court. Common swearing is forbidden, but civil oaths are permitted; self-defense is permitted, but not the taking of human life; ownership of property is permitted, but not the accumulation of wealth above one's needs. Self-denial, patience, humility, and prayer are identified as a Christian's responsibilities.

Only one sacrament is recognized, that of the Lord's Supper. Baptism, while having no regenerative power and inappropriate for infants, is recognized as an appropriate act for welcoming converts. This then, in brief, is a summary of the *Racovian Catechism*, accepted by common consent, not as a creed, but as the general standard of belief and conduct of the Minor Reformed Church of Poland. It was to remain essentially unchanged for the next sixty years.

United as never before and with new confidence and zeal, the church entered a period of vitality and growth. Raków became the center, not only of the church, but of great educational and scholarly activity. A school, established in 1602, grew rapidly, soon having a student body of approximately one thousand, one-third from the gentry. The press, established some years earlier, flourished, producing a constant stream of Socinian books and tracts. While always the smallest Protestant body in Poland, the Minor Church enjoyed significant growth during the first quarter of the seventeenth century. A general synod was held annually, with the ministers and lay leaders in attendance. The synod in 1611 at Raków attracted some 400 members, that in 1618 even more.

Although records are incomplete, Earl Morse Wilbur has estimated that overall there were at least 125 congregations—a few in cities or large towns, the rest in villages, on estates, or in rural locations. Ministers were expected to conduct daily prayers and to preach twice on Sunday as well as on Wednesday and Friday. Worship services ordinarily opened with a hymn and prayer, followed by a scripture reading and sermon. A concluding hymn and prayer were followed by an examination of the young people on the main points of the sermon.

The Lord's Supper was celebrated four times a year, on Christmas, Easter, Pentecost, and the Sunday after Michaelmas (September 29). In preparation, members were expected to reflect individually and communally on their faithfulness to disciplined Christian living. In fact, it was the high standard of morality expected of its members that undoubtedly kept the Minor Church from becoming larger.

But even as the church was flourishing, factors were at work in the larger culture that were to bring about its ruin. The Confederation of Warsaw with its guarantee of religious freedom was dependent on the integrity of the king and the compliance of all parties. Never consistently honored, it was soon to be ignored.

The Persecution and Destruction
of the Socinian Church

*How great a flood of fatal calamities from every
quarter overflowed all [Poland] during fourteen
years of confusion and savage wars, they cannot but
know who know at all what has taken place in
Europe in recent years. . . . And in that most unfortunate land always doubly unfortunate have been
and are the people of the [Socinian] Church. . . . For
we also had to struggle with these public calamities,
so many and great in comparison with those in
former times, and with the private enmities, even
more dangerous, of adversaries who supported the
party of the Pope of Rome.*

—JONAS SZLICHTYNG ET AL.
IN A LETTER OF THE UNITARIAN EXILES
JUNE 17, 1661

$\mathcal{O}$n the morning of December 16, 1611, Iwan Tyszkiewicz, a
member of the Minor Church, was beheaded in the great
marketplace of Warsaw as a rebel. Prior to the execution his
tongue had been cut out as a punishment for blasphemy;
afterward, since he had been convicted of throwing a crucifix
on the ground, one hand and foot were cut off; and finally,
since he had been convicted of heresy, his body was burnt.

Tyszkiewicz was a prominent citizen of Bielsk in Podlasie,
a town about one hundred miles east of Warsaw near White
Russia. He had incurred the enmity of both Orthodox and
Roman Catholics by leaving the Russian Orthodox Church to
become an ardent Socinian, as the members of the Minor

Church henceforth will be referred to. Moreover, when he came into a sizable inheritance, their anger was augmented by jealousy, and they sought a way to deprive him of his new wealth. Accordingly, they maneuvered him into accepting a position as the town's public steward, purposely not requiring him to take an oath of office, which he undoubtedly would have declined to do on religious grounds. Then when his term was over, they demanded that he swear he had performed his duties faithfully. This at first he refused to do, but in the end he consented to take the oath in the name of God and Christ, though not in the name of the Trinity nor upon the crucifix which had been presented him.

A few days later he was summoned to court and questioned by a priest, who became so angered by Tyszkiewicz's answers that he struck him and had him put in jail. When the case was resumed, friends of the accused protested that the actions of the court and priest were in violation of the Confederation of Warsaw. The judge ignored their objections, but they appealed the court's actions to a tribunal, which ordered the prisoner to be released and the prosecutors to pay a heavy fine. The judge, however, remanded the case to the king's court at Warsaw with the accusations now significantly altered— charging that Tyszkiewicz had thrown a crucifix to the ground, had blasphemed God, and had inflicted insults and great injury upon the court by appealing the case.

The king's court, after hearing the evidence, sent the case back with a recommendation of leniency, but Tyszkiewicz was nevertheless ordered to sell his property and leave town within six weeks under pain of death. Appeal of the sentence was made to the king's court, where it appears that the queen, a fervent Catholic in whose domain the town lay, used her influence to have the local court's actions sustained and the prisoner put to death as part of a fourfold sentence. His life would have been spared if he had renounced his heretical beliefs, but he remained firm in his convictions and went with nobility to an ignoble death. Thus Iwan Tyszkiewicz can be considered the first martyr of Unitarianism as an organized movement.

The Socinians already should have realized that the protection of the Confederation of Warsaw on which they had so long relied, was rapidly being taken from them. The Catholic clergy, led by the Jesuits, had become relentless in their public pronouncements that the religious liberty guaranteed by the Confederation never was intended to apply to "Arians," whom they considered to be well outside the Christian pale. Even after Tyszkiewicz's execution, however, the Socinians, convinced of the correctness of their doctrine and encouraged by their numerical growth, had continued to promote their cause aggressively, even though their safety depended on their avoiding the attention of those in power.

As it was, Catholics were perpetrating violent acts against the Socinians (or Polish Brethren, as they have often been called) with increasing frequency. "Arian" funerals were being disrupted, graves desecrated, and ministers attacked with little or no consequences. In the city of Lublin, which was both a Socinian stronghold and the site of a Jesuit university, tensions continued to rise. Finally, in 1627, violence broke out, precipitated by a fight between Catholic students and Protestant mercenaries in a public house. A mob gathered, venting its anger indiscriminately against all Protestants, plundering their homes and destroying both the Socinian and Calvinist houses of worship. The local tribunal not only gave tacit approval to these acts, it outlawed both churches and imposed fines on their leaders, claiming they were responsible for the disturbance. Although these actions of the tribunal were later overturned, thenceforth the local authorities repeatedly harassed the Socinians and in 1635 ordered their church closed forever. The site of the meetinghouse fell into the hands of the Jesuits, with the remnants of the once strong congregation finding refuge on the estate of a wealthy nobleman outside the city.

Raków, the chief Socinian center, was to become the next target of Catholic aggression. During the seven decades of its existence it had grown into a city of some twenty or thirty thousand people, with several thriving industries, a renowned school, and a prolific press. In 1638 an incident occurred that gave the Catholics an excuse to act. Two noblemen, one Socinian, the other Catholic, had become engaged in a dispute over the boundary between their lands, and the Catholic, to spite the Socinian, had erected a crucifix near the disputed border close to the outskirts of the city.

One day, as a group of younger students from the school were taking a walk with their teachers, two of them threw rocks at the crucifix, breaking it down. Some Catholic laborers in the area observed the act and reported it to the parish priest, who in turn reported it to his bishop. Public meetings denounced this desecration, and emotions ran high. The Socinian nobleman and the boys' parents tried to make amends, but to no avail. At length the matter was brought to the attention of the king, who ordered an investigation. The teachers, who by now had been accused of participation in the crucifix's destruction, fled in terror; even the Socinian nobleman's offer of a site and financial support for a Catholic church in Raków failed to stem the growing tide of hostility.

Proper process was bypassed, and the Polish Senate, heavily Catholic in makeup, took control of the case. Its judgment was as severe as it was unjust: the school, allegedly the source of the trouble, was to be permanently destroyed; so, too, was the Raków press, along with any of its publications that could be located; all "Arians" were to leave the city within four weeks' time, under pain of death. Protests were of no avail, and the provisions of the judgment were carried out rigorously. The Socinian congregation tried to reestablish its church in a nearby village, but only a remnant remained. As one Socinian lamented, "the very eye of Poland was plucked out, the sanctuary and refuge of exiles, the shrine of religion and the muses." In 1640 the local bishop laid the cornerstone of a Catholic church on the site where, just a few months earlier, the Socinian church had stood.

Determined not to give up, the Socinians immediately convened a general synod at Kisielin, a city in the Ukraine some 200 miles east of Raków and the home of their strongest congregation in that region. Those attending decided, in effect, to establish Kisielin as the new center of their faith, by strengthening the school there to the level that had been achieved at Raków and through resuming the publications program. The location seemed well suited for this undertaking; there were many powerful Socinian nobles in the area, as well as numerous churches. Moreover, Eastern Orthodoxy, less hostile than Roman Catholicism, was the predominant religion. The Socinians sent representatives to the local Calvinist synod to recommend a political alliance on behalf of religious toleration, a proposal that the Calvinists unfortunately rejected. (The Calvinists and other Protestants in Poland were, a few generations later, to suffer much the same fate as the Socinians.)

Nevertheless, the Socinians continued to be confident that their views would in time prevail, and they resumed promoting their faith with enthusiasm. However, the rapid growth of Kisielin as the center of Socinian religion, education, and propaganda soon generated opposition from both Orthodox and Catholics. Some of the ministers and teachers who had served at Raków had been recruited for the new enterprise, but the Socinians' opponents charged that this constituted a violation of the judgment against the Racovians, as did their creation of another "Arian" school and their continued propagation of "Arian" beliefs. The case dragged on for several years, but in the end, as with Raków, the tribunal ordered the churches and school closed, their buildings burned, and the heretics banished. After less than six years the Kisielin venture had come to an end.

Despite these discouraging events, the work of the church continued to go forward. After all, Socinianism was still legally tolerated in Poland despite the judgments rendered against Raków and Kisielin. The Socianians continued to hold annual synods, ordain and appoint ministers, address the needs of individual churches and ministers, support promising ministerial students, and secretly print books. They established a college at Luclawice, the Socinian stronghold where Faustus Socinus had spent his last years. Located near the Hungarian border, it had an active relationship with the Transylvanian Unitarians and was to survive until Poland was overrun during a war with Sweden in the late 1650s.

Nevertheless, the restrictions being imposed against "Arians" by diets and tribunals continued to be tightened. By 1636 Socinians had been specifically excluded from the protection of the Confederation of Warsaw; by 1647 they had been prohibited from making converts; a year later "Arian" deputies had been denied the vote in the Polish Diet and nobles forbidden to acquire land or build churches. However, the death of the Socinian Church in Poland was not to come from strangulation in the hands of diets and tribunals; instead, it was to come from a series of fatal blows, the first delivered by a horde of marauding Cossacks.

In 1648, following years of oppression and unrest, the Cossack peasants of the Ukraine had revolted and for the next few years ravaged the land as far west as the Vistula (or Wisla in Polish), the river that bisects Poland as it flows north to the Baltic. They wiped out whole cities, plundered churches and estates indiscriminately, and tortured, raped, killed, or took into slavery many of those who did not flee. Fortunately, more than 1,000 Socinians managed to escape the onslaught, eventually finding refuge with their brethren in western Poland. Just when it appeared that the rebellion might be quelled, Poland's archenemy, Russia, came to the aid of the Cossacks, destroying those Socinian churches in Lithuania that had managed to survive.

Then, while Russia was invading Poland from the east, Sweden, ambitious to expand its territory, began an invasion from the north under the pretense of helping to repel the Russians and Cossacks. Soon the Swedish army was controlling many cities, and when the Socinians of the foothill country in the south were endangered by invaders from the east, they sought refuge in Kraków under Swedish protection. Not long after this, a spontaneous uprising against the invaders took place throughout the country; the king, who had fled, returned to his throne; and the invaders were forced to withdraw. After more than a decade of warfare, peace finally had been restored, but the Socinians, on returning to their homes, found little but devastation. Nevertheless, despite continued persecution, they began regathering their congregations and rebuilding their churches.

Almost at once, however, they suffered a cruel blow. In 1658, soon after the Swedish army had withdrawn, the Polish Senate proclaimed that all those who had collaborated with the Swedes during the occupation would be granted amnesty, with the exception of the "Arians." It claimed that not only had the "Arians" been more treasonable than the other collaborators (those who had sought refuge in Kraków were especially singled out), but that they were abominable heretics as well. Those who would not recant were to be banished from the kingdom.

That same year a second deliberative body, the Polish Diet, after invoking a long-neglected law, decreed that all duly convicted "Arians" who would not renounce their faith would be put to death; however, as an act of clemency it granted them three years in which to settle their affairs and leave the country. The Socinians, shocked by this double condemnation, appealed to the king, but without success; to make matters worse, the following year their grace period was reduced from three years to two. Samuel Przypkowski, one of the ablest Socinian leaders, described their plight in a letter to a Dutch supporter:

> We were not the only ones who suffered the hardships of these many wars. Yet when the rest were again taking breath, we were the only ones (exhausted by so many

wars as we were, and almost at the point of death), to be
hit by a peace more cruel than any war finished off.
Without any respite we struggled with adverse fortune,
so that it seemed that in afflicting us the preceding wars
had only been assisting the savagery of the peace that
followed them. . . . [I]n the oppression of our Brethren
the authority of the laws was not looked for. Armed
themselves and surrounded by armed bands, "sacrifi-
cial" Papists invaded the homes of the [Socinian] nobles,
plundering, burning, raping noble ladies, and used all
manner of violence without fear of punishment. Nay,
although the law against us had not yet been enacted,
the court of the Tribunal, on the basis of unfortunate
precedents, implemented its rigor against us.

Przypkowski continued:

At length the many unlawful persecutions of innocent
persons were succeeded by a law [i.e., the decree of
1658] that covered all these wrongs, and in a new,
unheard-of way by violently oppressing those who had
the right to intercede, entered into the body of our laws
as though through the throat of liberty. This, indeed, at
first seem superfluous. . . . However, being furnished
with new darts of injury, it not only gave the semblance
of legality to all outrages of both judges and private
persons, but also gave us over to the active hatred of our
enemies, stripped of all assistance from our friends and
well-wishers, and, as it were, bound and shackled. . . .

As the deadline of July 10, 1660, approached, the Socinians
made one last effort to avoid exile. They proposed that a
friendly conference on religion be held—this in the forlorn
hope that the Catholic leadership could be persuaded that the
differences between the two churches were too small to require such drastic action. The bishop gave his assent, and a

five-day meeting was held during which debate was carried on in a courteous and dignified manner. Andrew Wiszowaty, Faustus Socinus's grandson, was the chief spokesperson for the Socinians and clearly bested the Catholics in argument. Indeed, one of his opponents remarked afterward, "If all the devils were to come out of hell, they could not defend their religion more strongly than this one man." Wiszowaty had made such a fine impression that he was offered an estate and a generous annuity if he would convert to Catholicism; he refused and went on to become the foremost leader of the Socinians in exile. Although it failed to achieve its original goal, the conference had two positive results: the attitude of the Catholics was to a degree softened and some of the Socinians who had been wavering were renewed in their faith.

Nevertheless, a significant number of Socinians, faced with banishment, did renounce their faith and accept baptism into the Catholic Church. For those who were poor, there was, practically speaking, little choice; they simply did not have the means by which to resettle in a new country. Some of the nobility also recanted; the prospect of losing their comfortable lives was just too daunting. (It is noteworthy that some of the wives and daughters of those who capitulated stood firm in their faith and accepted the consequences.) Almost all those who went into exile suffered heavy financial losses, for although they had been given two years in which to sell their goods and property, the circumstances placed them at a great disadvantage. As Przypkowski reported:

> Very few were able to sell their property; and of those who did by far the greatest part were forced to sell splendid estates to the buyers at a small price or for almost nothing, since the unfairness of the bidders not only took advantage of the necessity and the danger that pressed upon the sellers, but also of the scarcity and lack of money which was in exceedingly short supply. . . . Would you have an example of such a sale?

A noble lady, patroness of the church at Dobryn, sold her dowry rights valued at more than a thousand thalers for barely three hundred florin. But some had to be content with a fifteenth, others with a twentieth part, and many at last with a bare hope and a promise to pay. This forced many of our Brethren to prefer to entrust our property to the good faith of friends. So with their properties broken up, or rather scattered, or given over to the control of others, the fathers of families with their wretched band of children or kinsfolk had to leave their native land.

Probably no more than a few hundred families actually went into exile; perhaps a thousand more who wished to leave lacked the means. Others, still wavering, were hiding out with friends. The largest exodus took place across the southern border, with a train of at least 380 men, women, and children, together with 200 wagons, setting out for Transylvania in the hope of settling among the Unitarians there. Hardly had they crossed the Carpathian Mountains into Hungary, however, when they were attacked and robbed by a band of roving soldiers, encouraged, it was rumored, by the Socinians' Polish enemies. A large part of the group, stripped of their possessions and indeed most of their clothes, retraced their steps, eventually making their way northward to East Prussia, which was no longer under Polish rule. The rest, numbering about 200, pressed on, and in 1661 reached Kolozsvár (Cluj), where they were warmly received by the Transylvanian Unitarians. Their troubles, however, were not at an end. Exhausted by their journey and weakened by severe weather, many succumbed to the plague and other illnesses until barely thirty survived. But eventually other exiles joined them, and in time four Polish-speaking congregations were organized. The Socinian church in Kolozsvár lasted until 1792; by then assimilation into the local culture was essentially complete.

A second group of exiles found haven in the Silesian town

of Kreuzburg, Germany, but twelve miles across Poland's western border; from there they secretly could return to settle their affairs and help those who had been forced to stay behind. The group's first minister was Andrew Wiszowaty, the man who had so effectively debated the Catholics in an attempt to void the decree of banishment. He had served a number of congregations in Poland with great effectiveness before the exile; after it, he proved a tower of strength to the Socinian diaspora, traveling extensively at great personal risk to minister to those both outside and within the Polish borders.

With financial help from the Dutch Remonstrants, a group of liberal Protestants, Kreuzburg was to serve as the center of the Socinian movement for several years. The church held two general synods there, initiated communications with scattered groups, planned the education of a new generation of ministers and ordered the publication of needed books. Slowly, however, members drifted away, and when in 1671 a Jesuit passing through town learned that Socinians were living there, he demanded their expulsion, and the authorities reluctantly complied.

A more lasting center for the exiles was established in and around Königsberg, a city on the Baltic in East Prussia. Samuel Przypkowski, whose account of the plight of the Socinians has been quoted previously, came to Königsberg soon after the decree of banishment from Poland had been passed. There he secured a position in the service of the governor, who was well disposed toward the Socinians; thus Przypkowski was well situated to pave the way for other exiles to join him. As their numbers grew, the Lutheran clergy grew apprehensive and urged that the existing laws against "Arians" be enforced. In response, the exiles, at a synod held in 1663, instructed Przypkowski to prepare a petition to the governing powers requesting a place where they might safely settle; they also appointed two ministers to serve the area, regularized their financial procedures, and made plans to collect the scattered records of their movement.

With their numbers continuing to rise, a second synod was held two years later, with delegates coming from as far away as Transylvania. The meeting attracted so much attention that the authorities, under Lutheran pressure, ruled that no more meetings could be held until further notice. At this point Przypkowski's petition was presented on behalf of the Unitarians, as they now preferred to be called. In it they stoutly denied that they were blasphemers as had been charged, asserted that they did not own either the Anabaptist or Arian name (Socinians had from the beginning rejected the Arian designation as theologically incorrect), stated that they were moral, law abiding citizens, and claimed that they deserved to find a home in Prussia. The petition ended with an eloquent plea for religious tolerance on the grounds that liberty of conscience is a gift of God. Its effect was positive; the exiles were allowed to stay in Prussia, at least for the time being, and Przypkowski was allowed to acquire the nearby village of Kasinowo, henceforth to be the center of Socinianism in Prussia.

On the last day of 1669 the governor died, and without his protection the exiles were again in jeopardy; almost at once an edict was posted announcing that they must leave the country within three years. The Socinians presented another petition, and in time an uneasy compromise was reached whereby the Socinians were allowed to remain provided they refrained from publicizing their beliefs. They soon established three churches, and private worship was conducted in numerous homes. But in a foreign land with a different tongue and without permission to spread their faith, the Socinians inevitably suffered a decline in numbers. By 1754 only ninety remained in the whole of Prussia; and in 1803 public worship ceased altogether.

The Socinians succeeded in organizing a few congregations in the German regions of Brandenburg and the Rhine Palatinate, but most of Germany was hostile to the exiles. There was a widespread fear that Socinian views, if left unrefuted and allowed to spread, would poison the minds of the people.

Socinian writings were carefully scrutinized; for a century and a half Lutheran scholars and seminarians wrote books and dissertations exposing the heresies they had discovered. But though condemned at the time, these unorthodox views doubtless provided a leaven for German Enlightenment thought.

Not surprisingly, the Dutch reaction to Socinianism was far more positive. Holland had a strong tradition of religious toleration; many Socinian scholars and students had studied there, and on several occasions the possibility of a union between the Polish Socinians and either the Dutch Remonstrants or the Mennonites had been considered. In the early seventeenth century, a controversy had broken out in the Reformed Church between the Calvinists and the Arminians, followers of the teachings of Jacobus Arminius. Some eighty ministers of the latter group ("Remonstrants" they were called, because they had remonstrated or protested against several points of official doctrine) were put into wagons and sent into exile across the border into Germany. The Socinians at once offered their support and invited the refugees to resettle in Poland. Resettlement proved unnecessary, for within a few years the Remonstrants were allowed to return to their homeland where they began organizing churches and a seminary for the training of their ministers.

The two groups had established friendly relations, and a half century later it was to be the Remonstrants who were welcoming Socinian exiles. During that fifty-year interval Socinianism had exerted a growing influence on Remonstrant thought, both through books and personal contacts. The Remonstrants, however, publicly distanced themselves from the Socinians to avoid suspicion of heresy; in this they were but partially successful. As for the Mennonites, there had always been a strong undercurrent of antitrinitarianism among them, so that when Socinian books made their way to Holland in the early part of the seventeenth century, they found a positive reception among many of that group as well.

Thus, when after 1660, Socinian exiles began making their

way to Holland, they found a warm reception in many quarters. The most prominent among these exiles was Socinus's grandson Andrew Wiszowaty, the courageous minister to the diaspora who, following his ministry to exiled Brethren in Germany, settled in Amsterdam in 1666. There was, in Holland, no real opportunity for him to establish new congregations—the number of exiles was too small. Hence his ministry took a new form as he devoted much of his time and energy to corresponding with his fellow religionists scattered throughout western and central Europe, giving them advice, encouragement, and religious guidance.

Wiszowaty's thinking took a new form as well. Realizing that times were changing theologically and that it was no longer responsible to base one's faith strictly on a literal interpretation of scripture, he began placing more and more reliance on reason. The mature product of his thought is given in a little book, *Rational Religion (Religio rationalis)*, published posthumously, in which he argued that reason can be both a source of religious truth and the arbiter in drawing religious conclusions. In this he was, of course, departing radically from the viewpoint of his grandfather, who was convinced that divine revelation as reported in scripture was the sole source of religious truth.

During his final years, Wiszowaty collaborated with others in preparing a significantly revised edition of the *Racovian Catechism*, the final version of which was published in Amsterdam in 1680. Its preface affirmed the evolutionary nature of religious belief: "We do not think that we need blush if our Church advances in some things. We ought not in every case to cry out, We believe, I stand fast in the ranks, here I plant my foot, I will not allow myself to be moved from here ever so little." The changes reflected both the new cultural milieu in which the Socinians found themselves and the results of theological discussions carried on with the Remonstrants, Mennonites, and others, including the Jewish philosopher Benedict Spinoza.

The chapter on the Person of Christ was strengthened; so, too, was the chapter on baptism, with a new importance attached to baptism by immersion. The death of Christ was treated as an atoning sacrifice rather than an example of how suffering should be born. Socinus's view that only the righteous would be resurrected was rejected; the new edition taught "a resurrection of both the just and the unjust—and the latter will be consigned to everlasting punishment, but the former admitted to everlasting life." While still pacifistic in tone, a more positive, cooperative attitude toward the state was adopted. Not surprisingly, given Wiszowaty's involvement, the new edition, unlike those of 1605 and 1619, regularly appealed to reason as well as revelation in supporting its positions. But despite these changes, the catechism retained most of the theology and spirit of the earlier editions; it was obviously still well rooted in the soil of Polish Socinianism.

Wiszowaty died in Amsterdam in 1678 at the age of seventy, his ministry and writing continuing right up until the end of his life. His two sons had followed in his footsteps by becoming ministers, thus continuing the family's strong commitment to a cause begun four generations earlier by their great-uncle Laelius. But for all practical purposes, Socinianism as an organized religious movement died with the sons' generation. A few scattered congregations like those at Kasinowo and Kolozsvár somehow managed to keep going for a while longer, but by the beginning of the nineteenth century the last Socinian church had closed its doors.

"Thus," wrote Earl Morse Wilbur, "ends the history, at once heroic and pathetic, of the Socinians in Poland, the simple Polish Brethren, who united with the widest doctrinal freedom the most eager missionary zeal and the most fervent piety, as they conscientiously tried to live strictly after the literal teachings of Jesus." Their work, however, was not in vain, for during the century and a half of its existence their church had played a crucial part in the promotion of the principles of freedom, reason, and tolerance in religion, and its influence was to persist, directly and indirectly, far into the future.

Francis Dávid and the
Rise of Unitarianism in Transylvania

*Whom God enlightened by His spirit must not be silent
and must not hide the truth.*

—FRANCIS DÁVID

*W*hen, in 1661, the little band of Socinian exiles arrived
in Kolozsvár, they were welcomed by members of a church
whose roots extended back for almost a century, for it was in
1568 that the Unitarian movement had begun in Transylvania.
Since the first exclusively antitrinitarian synod had been held
in Poland in 1565, the two movements had, for all practical
purposes, originated simultaneously.

That the Socinians sought haven among the Unitarians was
not surprising, for links between the two groups had existed
almost from the beginning: both initially had been influenced
by the writings of Michael Servetus; Giorgio Biandrata had
played an important role in the start of both movements; and
Faustus Socinus had come to Transylvania to mediate an
internal doctrinal dispute back in 1578. These initial contacts
were not without controversy, but over the years the relationships between the two groups had warmed: the Transylvanian
churches had for nearly a century recruited ministers, teachers, and even a superintendent from among the Polish Brethren, and in return they had sent many of their young men to
Socinian schools and colleges to learn Polish and complete
their education. Moreover, in Kolozsvár the exiles would qualify
for protection under the same laws that specifically guaranteed Unitarians religious toleration.

At the time of the outbreak of the Reformation in the early

sixteenth century, the population of Transylvania was largely Catholic, although the ties to Rome were weak and the Inquisition had never been established there. Three major ethnic groups co-existed with little intermingling: the Szeklers, Hungarian-speaking descendants of Hun invaders; the Magyars, descendants of Russian invaders and also Hungarian-speaking; and the Saxons, descendants of German immigrants. The Magyars were, for the most part, to remain loyal to Catholicism; the Saxons became converts to Lutheranism; while the Szeklers became either Calvinists or Unitarians.

Transylvania at one time had been on the main route between Western Europe and the near and far East, but after the Turks had begun to invade Europe in the sixteenth century, the route was abandoned as being too dangerous. Thereafter Transylvania, surrounded by mountains on all sides, became something of a forgotten land, while at the same time serving as a protective buffer between Western Europe and the East. Until 1545 it had comprised the eastern quarter of the old Kingdom of Hungary; thereafter, for a century and a half, it existed as an autonomous state.

Francis Dávid (Dávid Ferenc in Hungarian) was born at Kolozsvár in the first quarter of the sixteenth century (the date is uncertain), the son of a Magyar mother and a Saxon father. After an early education in Catholic schools, he was sent by wealthy patrons to study at Wittenberg, where he became acquainted with the ideas of the Reformation. By the time he returned to Transylvania, he found the Reformation well under way there, and Dávid, after serving briefly as rector of a Catholic school, renounced Catholicism to become a Lutheran minister. By 1555 he had become rector of a Lutheran school and minister of a congregation in Kolozsvár, and the following year he was appointed superintendent of the Hungarian-speaking Lutheran churches. For several years he defended the Lutheran position on the Lord's Supper (the "real presence" of Christ in the bread and wine) against that of the Calvinists (the Spirit's presence); but by 1559 he had become converted to the latter's position, at the same time hoping that the differences between the Protestant camps could be overcome and the two united.

Nevertheless the schism continued to grow, and with his country seriously divided, King John Sigismund was persuaded to convene a special ecclesiastical assembly or synod to attempt a resolution of the controversy. He chose Giorgio Biandrata, who had come from Poland to be his mother's physician and had gained his full confidence, to represent him at the meeting, which was held at the city of Enyed in April 1564. Neither side would compromise, however, and after the meeting the division between the Lutherans and the Calvinists was essentially complete. By the year's end Dávid had accepted the position of bishop of the Calvinist, or Reformed, churches.

Biandrata had been impressed by Dávid's debating skills and clear thinking at the Enyed synod and soon persuaded the king to appoint him as court preacher. Once the two had been thrown together it is probable that Biandrata began sharing his antitrinitarian views with Dávid, who himself already had expressed doubts concerning the Trinity. At any rate, Dávid's thinking was in the process of undergoing significant change, and it was not long before he began rejecting Calvinistic doctrine. No creedal standards had as yet been set for the Reformed churches, and thus the way lay open for theological change under Dávid's leadership.

In January 1566, Dávid preached his first Unitarian sermon in the main church in Kolozsvár and soon thereafter was publicly debating the trinitarian Protestants. Interest in doctrinal matters was running high at that time, and public debates between reform-minded and conservative preachers about "the old papal science and the new gospel" were becoming as popular as tournaments and jousts once had been. As one chronicler of the times put it, "One heard all over Transylvania in the villages and in cities, even among the ordinary people, the great disputes during meals, during drinking, in the evening and the morning, at night and daytime, in the common talk and from the pulpits, even accusations and fights between the representatives of the two religions."

Not surprisingly, the Calvinists in the region were upset by these developments. Peter Mélius, superintendent of the Reformed churches across the border in eastern Hungary, soon emerged as the chief spokesman for the orthodox, denouncing Dávid's views as heretical. He was further inflamed when Dávid and Biandrata published a book, *The False and True Knowledge of God*, setting forth their position and showing clear evidence of Servetus's influence. (That Servetus's writings had circulated in Transylvania is quite obvious; in fact, one of the three existing copies of *The Restoration of Christianity* was once the property of a Transylvanian nobleman.)

Particularly galling to the Calvinists were eight pictures in the book, included as visual representations of the Trinity. One depicted Father, Son, and Holy Spirit as three men seated at a table; another showed a three-headed figure sitting on an altar. Even though all were taken from orthodox sources, they were condemned as blasphemous, included only to ridicule Christianity in general and the Calvinists in particular. Mélius responded by calling a synod of the Reformed ministers in Hungary "to take action against the heresies of Sabellius, Arius, Paul of Samosata, Photinus, and their like," challenging Dávid, Biandrata, and their followers to attend and defend their position or else to be proclaimed as defeated. The challenge was not accepted; the Unitarians suspected that once they were on Hungarian soil they might be arrested and imprisoned as heretics.

Early in 1568, King John Sigismund, concerned to end the religious controversy that was dividing his country, convened a diet at Torda during which previous decrees of religious toleration were reaffirmed and the principle of toleration further strengthened. Dávid was particularly eloquent on this occasion, and copies of a picture of him addressing the Diet of Torda have graced the walls of Unitarian churches in Transylvania down to the present day. Following a unanimous vote of the diet, the king issued the following Act of Religious Tolerance and Freedom of Conscience:

> His Majesty, our Lord, in what manner he—together with his realm [i.e., the Diet]—legislated in the matter of religion at the previous Diets, in the same manner now, in this Diet, reaffirms that in every place the preachers shall preach and explain the Gospel each according to his understanding of it, and if the congregation like it, well, if not, no one shall compel them for their souls would not be satisfied, but they shall be permitted to keep a preacher whose teaching they approve. Therefore none of the superintendents or others shall abuse the preachers, no one shall be reviled for his religion by anyone, according to the previous statutes, and it is not permitted that anyone should threaten anyone else by imprisonment or by removal from his post for his teaching, for faith is the gift of God, this comes from hearing, which hearing is by the word of God.

Shortly thereafter, in a further attempt to promote unity, the king convened a general synod at the capital in Gyulafehérvár at which Dávid, Biandrata, and their followers defended the unity of God, while Mélius and his followers (and, in addition, the Lutheran Saxons) defended the Trinity. The meeting was held in the palace, with the king—who firmly believed in debate as the best means for resolving differences—present as a highly interested observer. Proceedings began each day at five o'clock in the morning, and although the atmosphere was tense and feelings often ran high, the debate was carried out with reasonably good order. The arguments were based almost entirely on interpretation of scripture, with representatives of the two sides speaking alternately. Biandrata at first took an active part, but soon realized that he was out of his depth and let Dávid take over leadership by himself.

After ten days the king adjourned the meeting, withholding judgment on which side had prevailed until fuller and clearer opinions could be offered. Determined to promote tranquillity, he ordered both sides, under threat of severe penalty, to refrain from quarreling or abusing each other, either verbally or in writing. "The disputation," wrote one orthodox historian, "began with heat, lasted not too temperately for ten days, and closed without any profit accruing to the church of Christ."

But despite the claims of the trinitarians, the debate was generally regarded as a victory for Dávid and his followers. According to tradition, a great throng greeted Dávid as he entered Kolozsvár, whereupon he mounted a boulder and preached the unity of God with such power that the people carried him on their shoulders to the great church on the square. There, it was said, he continued with such eloquence that the whole city accepted the Unitarian faith then and there!

In actuality, Dávid and his followers found their position at this point to be far from secure. Harsh attacks by the trinitarian camp continued, with threats made of a death penalty for heretics; the Unitarians countered by defending their position through a steady flow of publications. It appears that by then the whole country was in a state of confusion with regard to religion. As a result, King John called for yet another debate between the two warring factions, this one to be held at Várad and conducted in Hungarian rather than Latin in order that the common people could better understand the arguments. Debate was to be restricted to four topics: Who is the one God? Who is the only-begotten Son of God the Father? Concerning the Holy Spirit; and concerning the divinity of Christ.

Dávid and Mélius led their parties; Biandrata, unable to speak Hungarian, did not take part. The proceedings lasted for six days, with the king and his court in attendance. At one point the king, apparently annoyed by Mélius's tactics, interrupted the proceedings to state that "Inasmuch as we know that *faith is the gift of God*, and that conscience cannot be forced, if one cannot comply with these conditions, let him go beyond the Tisza," that is, leave this country and go to Hungary. Dávid then spoke powerfully in defense not only of his party's doctrinal position but of religious toleration as well.

When the debate ended the king expressed regret that the unity he sought could not be reached and ordered Mélius to desist from attacking Dávid and his followers since "we demand in our dominion freedom of conscience." By then, he and most of his court had been won over to Dávid's side. As one opponent later put it, "Certainly the whole trinitarian Christian world could have furnished no man who could cope with the Unitarians, not in abuse, but on grounds of Scripture and reason that could by no means be refuted." This proved to be the last great debate between the two parties of the Reformed Church in Transylvania; thereafter they pulled ever further apart.

The effect of the Várad debate was both immediate and profound. Many Transylvanians were quite ready to follow their king in accepting Dávid's position, and Unitarianism, with its rallying cry of "*Egy az Isten*" ("God is One") soon became the leading faith in the land. As evidence of this rapid growth, a Unitarian synod held in 1577 attracted 322 ministers, and by 1595 the number of churches had grown to more than 525. Nevertheless, during the years immediately following Várad the movement was in some disarray, with no legal status, no doctrinal standards, and little organizational structure. Moreover, King John, whose support had been so critical, was in precarious health; should he die, the future of the whole movement might be in jeopardy.

Accordingly, Dávid and other Unitarian leaders persuaded the king to bring the matter of their churches' status before the diet. This was done, and in January 1571, Unitarianism was formally recognized as one of the country's "received reli-

gions," enjoying equal constitutional status with Roman Catholicism, Calvinism, and Lutheranism. This recognition came
just in time; it was to save the Unitarians in Transylvania from
suffering the same fate that would later befall their Socinian
counterparts in Poland. The securing of this recognition was to
be King John Sigismund's last public act; the day after the
diet adjourned, while on his way to a hunting exposition with
Dávid and Biandrata, he was seriously injured when his carriage
overturned. Shortly thereafter he became mortally ill, dying in
March at the age of thirty, the only Unitarian king in history.

The king had died without leaving an heir, and out of the
ensuing confusion emerged a new ruler, Stephen Báthory. His
election by the diet was in part to maintain peaceful relations
with Transylvania's near neighbors, Hungary on the west and
Turkey on the south. Under a new treaty Transylvania came
partially under Hungarian control, and Báthory was given the
title of prince, not king. The new ruler was a Roman Catholic
and, although friendly toward the Protestants, he also was
concerned to slow the growth of Unitarianism in his domain.
He imposed censorship, closed down the Unitarian press, and
dismissed from court positions all Unitarians except Biandrata,
who was retained as the prince's physician and legal advisor.
Dávid, of course, was replaced as court preacher. While the
diet in 1572 reconfirmed King John's decree of religious freedom, it also passed, on Prince Stephen's initiative, a new law
forbidding any innovation in religion; any changes in doctrine or practice were, it was felt, likely to cause civil unrest.
A few years later Prince Stephen was chosen to fill the Kingdom of Poland's vacant throne; thereafter he ruled Transylvania
in absentia, turning over most of the responsibilities to his
brother Christopher.

Francis Dávid, meanwhile, was going through a difficult
time. No longer was he an influential member of the royal
court; the closing of the Unitarian press had restricted his
opportunity to promulgate his views; the passage of the law
against innovation posed a threat against refinement of his

doctrines; and, moreover, his marriage had ended in divorce. Particularly humiliating was the fact that the divorce proceedings were settled by a Calvinist court, since the Unitarians had no official superintendent and were not sufficiently well organized to have a court of their own. The case did, however, bring the need for greater organization to the Unitarians' attention. As a result they petitioned the diet, which in 1576 decreed "that those brethren that are of the religion of Francis Dávid may have Francis Dávid for their superintendent, and if he dies or becomes ill, or is for any other reason replaced, they may replace him and substitute another with the same authority; provided only that in the matter of religion he shall introduce no innovation, but it shall remain in the state in which he found it." (It was not until 1600 that the name "Unitarian" first came into use; in the early stages of their movement they, like the Polish Socinians, preferred to be called simply "Christians.")

Dávid, anxious to develop further his movement's doctrinal system, sought to soften through ecclesiastical means the impact of the law against innovation. The well-attended Unitarian synod held at Torda in 1578 passed a resolution "which gave all the ministers liberty without danger to discuss with one another and to investigate matters that have not yet been decided and settled by the general synod, but to which serious consideration might be given . . . in good order under rules suited to our times." Soon afterward, Dávid—protected, as he thought, by this resolution—began meeting with other ministers in his home, raising for discussion questions such as the following: Could Christ, since he was not called God by the Apostles, positively be called God? Could Christ properly be invoked in prayer? Were the doctrines of justification and predestination as taught by Luther and Calvin believable? Could Jesus still have been Christ had he not died? Dávid had, of course, already arrived at answers to some of the questions he raised but apparently wished to refine his own thinking and that of others on such matters.

When news of these discussions reached Biandrata at the royal court, he wrote Dávid, advising him not to bring up such questions at the next synod lest he be accused of innovation. Dávid heeded the warning as far as the synod was concerned, but he continued addressing the questions, not only in his home but also from his Kolozsvár pulpit. Confident that he possessed the truth and relying on the protection of the resolution, he publicly put forth the thesis that since Christ was not God, he should not be invoked in prayer. Biandrata responded in disagreement, but Dávid continued to affirm his position. At length Biandrata, alarmed that Dávid might be found guilty of innovation and the whole Unitarian movement destroyed, wrote to Faustus Socinus in Basel, urging him to come to Transylvania and try to convince Dávid of the error of his position; all his expenses would be paid. Socinus, as reported earlier, had by this time begun to emerge as the leading theologian of the antitrinitarian movement; he was soon to settle permanently in Poland and become the acknowledged leader of the Polish Brethren.

Socinus arrived in Kolozsvár in November 1578, taking up residence in Dávid's home as a paying guest. For more than four months the two men debated points of doctrine, especially over the issue of the invocation and worship of Christ. The main lines of debate eventually were put into writing, with Dávid defending from scripture the following four theses:

1. The strict command of God is that no one is to be invoked save God the Father, Creator of heaven and earth;
2. Christ, the teacher of truth, taught that no one is to be invoked beside the heavenly Father;
3. True invocation is defined as that which is paid to the Father in spirit and in truth;
4. The forms of simple prayer are directed not to Christ but to the Father.

Socinus refuted Dávid's arguments at length, with Dávid responding at even greater length. They finally agreed that all these written materials would be forwarded to the Polish Brethren for their judgment, after which the whole matter would be placed before a general synod for a final decision. Dávid, however, convened a synod even before the materials had been sent. It was necessary, he claimed, for the work of the Unitarian churches to go on; ministers needed to be ordained and moral abuses among the clergy to be corrected. The synod, though, went well beyond such housekeeping tasks in its deliberations. It adopted articles maintaining that to refine existing doctrines in order to free them of superstition and error did not constitute innovation; further, that the natural consequence of belief in the one God was that he alone should be worshiped. Biandrata was angered by what had taken place, claiming that Dávid had broken agreed-upon rules by initiating these latter actions before the reply from the Polish Brethren had been received. Soon the friendship between the two men who had initiated the Unitarian movement in Transylvania came to a bitter end; thereafter there was only enmity between them.

On the Sunday following the synod, Dávid, emboldened by its actions, preached a sermon to his congregation in which he declared that invoking Christ in prayer was no better than the Catholic practice of worshiping the Virgin Mary or the dead saints. The outspokenness of his message doubtless threw the congregation into consternation, since the invocation of Christ was still a common practice among Dávid's followers. Biandrata was now quick to inform Prince Stephen of what was taking place, and the latter ordered that Dávid be placed under house arrest until the matter could be properly investigated. On hearing this, but before the order could be carried out, Dávid preached again, telling the congregation why he was being arrested. He concluded by declaring, "Whatever the world may yet try to do, it will nevertheless become clear to the whole world that God is one." It was to be his last sermon.

In early June 1579, the prince convened a diet at Gyulafehérvár to try the case. As Dávid left Kolozsvár to attend his trial, a large crowd of supporters accompanied him to the city's gate where he bid them a tearful farewell; by the time the three-day journey was over, he was so ill and weak that he scarcely could stand. The trial was conducted in the great hall of the palace in the presence of the prince, Dávid's trinitarian accusers, and a panel of noblemen who served as judges. Socinus was present but did not participate; he was soon to return to Poland. (Incidentally, the response from the Polish Brethren, when it was received, not surprisingly upheld Socinus's position; for them, the invocation of Christ had become the ultimate test of one's being a Christian.)

Biandrata, as the prince's chief counsel, led the prosecution, professing great regret at having to assume this role and pointing out that he had repeatedly warned Dávid not to continue on the course he was taking. There followed an inquiry into Dávid's teachings, but Dávid's son-in-law, Lucas Trauzner, reminded the court that it was not the validity of those teachings that was being questioned, but whether they were new. Biandrata then accused Dávid of returning to Judaism by refusing to invoke Christ, to which Dávid replied that Biandrata himself had once held the same position. This Biandrata denied and urged that Dávid's four theses be read, with Trauzner again objecting that they had no relevance to the case. The defense then requested adjournment because of Dávid's weak condition; this was granted, though over Biandrata's angry objection.

When court reconvened the following day, Dávid was too weak to walk and was carried into the hall on a chair. He was, however, able to speak in his own defense, submitting evidence to show that he had held the views under dispute long before the innovation law was passed and that indeed Biandrata and other of his accusers had held these views as well. After the defense rested, Dávid was removed from the hall while his trinitarian accusers were permitted to stay; they all solemnly swore that they had never held Dávid's opinions. When Dávid was brought back to hear the decision, Biandrata gave him what later was termed "a Judas embrace," bade him to be of good courage, and promised his support. One Calvinist minister present urged the prince to impose the death penalty, but Dávid's other accusers urged that his life be spared—that he was guilty of innovation seems to have been a foregone conclusion.

Three days later the prince pronounced punishment; Dávid was condemned to life imprisonment. He was taken to the castle at Déva and placed in a dungeon cell where he soon died, probably in mid-November 1579; it is not known where his body was buried. Trauzner, who had stood loyally by his father-in-law's side to the very end of the trial, narrowly missed sharing the same fate. He managed to escape to Hungary, however, and there became a lawyer. Returning to Transylvania twenty-four years later, he was arrested and himself imprisoned in Déva, being released only after accepting the Catholic faith.

Controversy over the trial began at once and has continued down through the years. On the one hand, Dávid was evidently convinced that doctrinal reform was too important to postpone because of a threat of punishment that might never materialize; confident in the rightness of his cause, neither a law nor an agreement deterred him. Biandrata, on the other hand, having failed to dissuade Dávid from his dangerous course, apparently felt it necessary to turn against his friend and coreligionist in order to save the Unitarian movement from destruction; that he considered an agreement to have been broken would, of course, have made this easier to do. With neither man willing to give in to the other, a showdown was inevitable.

It would appear, leaving personalities aside, that the trial for the most part was conducted fairly, and based on the evidence, the verdict of innovation seems neither unreasonable nor surprising. Most Unitarians in Transylvania, then and now, have taken Dávid's side and roundly denounced Biandrata's actions. Indeed, two years after the trial, *A Defense of Francis Dávid (Defensio Francisci Davidis)* was published supporting Dávid's course of action and accusing Biandrata of carrying out a diabolical plot against him for personal reasons. Whatever the proper judgment of the case may be, Dávid quickly emerged as a martyr-hero, the founder and inspirer of the Unitarian movement.

Francis Dávid was still in the process of working out a complete doctrinal system at the time of his imprisonment, thus much remained unfinished. The cornerstone of his system, however, was solidly in place. He had early focused on the unqualified unity of God as being central. "God is indivisible," he had preached, and it was this emphasis that gave the Transylvanian Unitarians their rallying cry of *"Egy az Isten"* ("God is One"). In his last sermon he reaffirmed some of his basic beliefs:

> I believe in one God, who is not a trinity, but that Father from whom all exist and we are in him. . . . In this one most high God, Christ's Father, creator of heaven and earth we believe with strong faith. . . . We believe in Jesus Christ, our only Lord, by whom all exist, the most high God's son, who is man, born of King David's seed . . . and his being God's son had been proven. . . . We do not confess him being God either in his essence or in his person. . . . We believe in the holy spirit as being the spirit of the Father and the son . . . which comes from the Father and through the son to believers.

All this and more Dávid had worked out through a rational interpretation of scripture, in the course of which he had rejected the Trinity, affirmed God's unity and likewise the humanity of Christ. For Dávid, God was no abstract formulation but rather a loving Father from whom everything comes—

wise, infinite, the source of light and truth—and Christ was the human conduit through which God is made known to humanity. Given this understanding of Christ, it is not surprising that Dávid held a positive view of humanity, seeing it as evolving in the direction of the perfection made manifest in Jesus. The Holy Spirit he regarded, not as an objective entity, but rather as the power emanating from God that permeates the whole creation and that comes to humanity through Christ—"the power of the divine nature and life which is poured into us, so we don't live by *our* life any more but [rather] according to God-given life."

Salvation comes, he maintained, not through a vicarious atonement, but through faith in God and Christ and through the deeds that such faith inspires. Dávid's preaching was by his own admission theoretical rather than practical; for example, he paid little attention to the ethical lessons to be found in the parables of Jesus or the Sermon on the Mount in the Gospel of Matthew. It was necessary, he contended, to first work out a consistent and true doctrinal system, then the rest would follow. Nor had he concerned himself much with questions concerning the afterlife or the miracles portrayed in the Gospels. His strong objection to the invocation and worship of Christ—an objection that ultimately cost him his freedom and his life—was, of course, an inevitable consequence of his understanding of the nature of God.

Dávid's confidence that he had been enlightened by God's spirit and that his views were true had given him the courage to press on, while at the same time blinding him to the probable consequences. Had he lived and been given freedom, he doubtless would have continued much further with the doctrinal reformation that he had begun. As it was, he was confident to the end that this reformation would continue, for inscribed on the wall of his dungeon cell was found the following message: "Neither the sword of popes, nor the cross, nor the image of death—nothing will halt the march of truth. I wrote what I felt and that is what I preached with trusting spirit. I am convinced that after my destruction the teachings of false prophets will collapse."

Transylvanian Unitarianism:
Its Persistence Through Travail

My friends, be adaptable. The condition of our continued survival is constant adaptation.

—DEMETRIUS HUNYADI

Sisters and brothers, we are a tiny flock, yet quality cannot be replaced by quantity. A handful of quality people represent greater value than an entire army of faint hearts.

—GEORGE ENYEDI

*A*lthough Francis Dávid's spirit and example were to survive and inspire the Unitarians of Transylvania through future generations, the immediate impact of his imprisonment and death was devastating. Giorgio Biandrata, as their most prominent lay leader, was quick to impose his command, summoning all the ministers who had supported Dávid to appear before the prince at Gyulafehérvár. Threatened with the same fate that had befallen their leader, they were forced to renounce his opinions; then a month later Biandrata convened a general synod at Kolozsvár where all were required to subscribe to a doctrinal statement presumably based on those views generally held prior to the innovation law.

The statement consisted of four articles, affirming the divinity, worship, invocation, and kingdom of Christ. Regulations were adopted forbidding public or private debate and sermons on controversial subjects; establishing the Lord's Prayer, the Lord's Supper, and infant baptism as regular practices; and requiring all ministers to attend synods regularly. In addition, a consistory, or council, of twenty-four ministers was chosen to assist the new superintendent in overseeing the affairs of the churches. Since Biandrata's choice for the super-intendency, Demetrius Hunyadi, failed to receive the synod's support, he simply withdrew the nomination and had Hunyadi appointed to the position directly by the prince.

Soon thereafter, the reply from the Polish Brethren was received, upholding, as noted earlier, Faustus Socinus's views on the invocation of Christ rather than Dávid's. Biandrata delivered the reply to the newly formed consistory, which in turn distributed copies to the ministers for their study. A general synod was then convened at Kolozsvár in early 1580 at which all but sixteen or eighteen of the 250 ministers present subscribed to the Polish Brethren's conclusion. Those who did not were forbidden to preach until their case could be decided at a future synod. It is evident from subsequent writings that Dávid's position had far greater support than the numbers indi-cated; many ministers evidently were bowing to expediency in the face of the law against innovation. A number of them, unwilling to compromise their integrity, relocated across the border to serve Unitarian churches in eastern Hungary.

Despite his apparent successes, Biandrata's leadership proved to be short-lived. Faced with resentment and anger over his role in Dávid's conviction, he soon withdrew from the Unitarian movement altogether, though continuing to serve as physician in the prince's largely Catholic court until his death. His allegiance to Unitarianism, though hidden, evidently remained; his estate was left to his nephew, on the condition that he remain true to the Unitarian faith.

The choice of Hunyadi as superintendent proved to be a good one. Dávid had been an inspirational rather than an institutional leader; his interests had been theological, not administrative, and many of the churches had fallen into disarray. Hunyadi, on the other hand, was an effective admin-istrator who had served for six years as rector of the college at Kolozsvár before his appointment to the superintendency. As superintendent he divided the churches into twelve districts, each with its own dean; convened annual synods designed to bring about better organization and to strengthen the religious education of the children; and with Jesuits beginning to invade the country, willingly confronted them in debate.

Despite his hard and effective work, he was never, as Dávid's successor, able to attain popularity; in time, however, he overcame much of the hostility directed at him as Biandrata's hand-picked choice for the superintendency. Hunyadi served in that capacity for almost thirteen years, during which time the Unitarian movement slowly recovered. After Dávid's imprisonment and death, many people—nobles and common folks alike—who had been attracted to his cause had fallen away, and the ministers who had been forced to disown his views remained deeply resentful. Nevertheless, under Hunyadi's careful leadership the movement recovered, at least numerically. When he died suddenly in 1592, after being stricken while preaching in the great church at Kolozsvár, over 400 Unitarian churches existed in Transylvania.

Fortunately, an able replacement was found in the person of George Enyedi, who was quickly named to fill the position. Like Hunyadi, he had served as rector of the college at Kolozsvár, earning a reputation for brilliant scholarship. His book *Explicationes*, published posthumously, contradicted the arguments supporting the Trinity and was considered so dangerous to the orthodox position that it was banned throughout the empire; all copies that fell into trinitarian hands were publicly burnt. Unlike Hunyadi, Enyedi was unencumbered by the weight of being Dávid's successor and soon established himself as a popular champion of the Unitarian cause. His superintendency came at an extremely difficult time in Transylvanian history, for both Prince Stephen Báthory and his brother Christopher had died, and the latter's son Sigismund had assumed the throne in 1581 at the age of nine. Political chaos soon followed, encouraged by Jesuits who had entered the country determined to overthrow the Protestant-dominated diet and establish a new government under Catholic control.

In August 1594, the young prince, now twenty-three, invited the members of the diet, then convened at Kolozsvár, to meet with him that they might accompany him to divine worship. Once assembled, the group was surrounded by soldiers, with thirteen seized and placed under arrest. The following day five of the thirteen, all of them Unitarians, were charged with conspiracy, taken to the marketplace, and beheaded; four others were privately strangled, and the rest banished from the country. It was to be the beginning of nearly two centuries of almost uninterrupted persecution of the Transylvanian Unitarians: for a decade under a Catholic emperor, then for nearly the whole of the seventeenth century under a succession of Calvinist princes, and finally through most of the eighteenth under the Catholic monarchs of Austria. Moreover, for this entire period the Unitarians were prevented by law from carrying their theological reformation further. To reject the Trinity, affirm God's unity, and assert Christ's humanity was as far as they could go. To have gone that far had brought them oppression; to have gone further undoubtedly would have brought them annihilation.

With his chief opponents out of the way and their wealth confiscated, Prince Sigismund quickly entered into a treaty with Rudolph II, emperor of the Holy Roman Empire, transferring to him sovereignty over Transylvania; thus was the way laid for the beginning of the Catholic Counter-Reformation. Francis Dávid had had a foreboding of what was to happen. "I can see that the Prince [Stephen] means to bring in the Jesuits," he would tell a friend, "and hence I often warn my ministers to be on their guard lest they be overcome by them; but they will not listen to me." The emperor wasted no time in sending General George Básta, an Italian soldier notorious for his cruelty, to rule Transylvania as his military governor. For over five years Básta conducted a reign of terror, seizing Protestant churches and either burning them or turning them over to the Catholics, killing many of their ministers, and threatening with death every Protestant who refused to convert to Catholicism.

Finally in 1602 there was a general revolt against Básta's oppressive rule, led by a heroic Unitarian, Mózes Székely. With Turkish aid Mózes and his followers succeeded in capturing control of part of Transylvania, driving Básta's troops out of Kolozsvár along with the Jesuits who had taken over the church and college. In 1603 a diet held at Gyulafehérvár chose Mózes as the country's new prince, with the Turkish sultan confirming his election. Básta rallied his forces, however, surprising Mózes's army in a night attack in which Mózes and many of the Transylvanian noblemen were killed. The whole country was then laid waste by fire and sword, and the devastation was followed by a dreadful famine in which many died. People resorted to eating raw roots and herbs and the flesh of dogs, cats, and horses. No draft animals remained, and what plowing took place was by plows drawn by teams of ten men. In some places, cannibalism even broke out.

Básta singled out the Unitarians for his most savage reprisals, destroying their remaining churches, forbidding their public worship, fining and taxing their people to the point of ruin, and returning to Jesuit control the church and college at Kolozsvár. He had planned to have the superintendent, Matthew Toroczkai, put to death, but the latter saved himself by hiding in an iron mine where, in an act of hope, he composed hymns to be sung once the oppression was over. (George Enyedi, who had been superintendent when the turmoil had started and had witnessed the 1594 executions, had died an early death, brought on in part by stress.)

Fortunately, a second and more successful revolt against Básta's regime soon took place. It was led by a Hungarian nobleman and military officer, Stephen Bocskai, who united Transylvanians of all classes behind him and with the help of Turkish forces drove Básta from the country. Unanimously elected prince by the diet in 1605, he negotiated a peace treaty

with Rudolph II, expelled the Jesuits, restored religious freedom, and returned to the Unitarians their churches and schools.
Under the leadership of Toroczkai the Unitarians then struggled
back to something approaching a normal existence. They
resumed holding annual synods, prepared a hymnal for the
first time (evidently Toroczkai's efforts in the iron mine had
born fruit), and published in Hungarian both Enyedi's
Explicationes and the newly completed *Racovian Catechism*.
The publication of the latter indicated a growing acceptance of
Socinian views by the Unitarians, thwarted as they were by the
innovation law from extending Dávid's more daring thought.

But once again the Unitarians' respite from oppression was
short-lived. Starting in 1608 a succession of Calvinist princes,
the first a convert from Catholicism, ruled the land. Even
though each in turn had sworn on accession to the throne to
preserve the rights of all four "received religions" (Catholicism, Lutheranism, Calvinism, and Unitarianism), they nevertheless found ways to restrict Unitarian worship and to dis-
place ministers from their pulpits. Moreover, a crisis soon
developed in the country that was to further hurt the Unitarian cause. A Sabbatarian movement had begun in the late
sixteenth century as an outgrowth of Christianity, with its
followers stressing the absolute unity of God and the humanity of Jesus as the promised Messiah. Its most conspicuous
mark was the observance of the seventh day of the week as the
Sabbath, but its followers also observed Old Testament customs and dietary laws, none of which, they claimed, had ever
been abrogated. Not belonging to one of the recognized received religions, the Sabbatarians worshiped and observed
their customs in private while at the same time claiming
membership in one of the recognized faiths. Although a few
claimed to be Catholics or Calvinists, the vast majority, not
surprisingly, were registered as Unitarians.

Over the years the movement had grown in strength and
inevitably had come to public attention, being commonly
perceived as more Jewish than Christian. In 1618 the Calvinist

prince decided to intervene. He authorized János Keserüi Dajka, the superintendent of the Reformed (Calvinist) churches, to enforce rigidly a recently enacted law against Sabbatarianism. Dajka directed his efforts primarily at the Unitarians, who long had been accused of holding Sabbatarian views. In fact, as early as 1583 the Jesuits had been planting seeds of suspicion by reporting that the Unitarians of Kolozsvár were forsaking the Christian gospel for the prophecies of the Old Testament and that "the Unitarian ministers . . . universally abstain from blood and pork," thus allegedly following Jewish dietary laws.

Dajka began his task by compelling the official boards of the Unitarian churches to declare that Sabbatarians were not properly members and forever were excluded from fellowship. Then all those identified as Sabbatarians were given the choice of converting to Calvinism or suffering severe penalties; faced with these alternatives, some fled the country. The overall losses to the Unitarian cause were significant; many, either accused or merely suspected of holding Sabbatarian views, became Calvinists out of expediency. The Unitarian churches were handicapped during this crisis by having at that time a superintendent who, being Polish, was unacquainted with the language and thus unable to provide efficient leadership.

It appeared for a time that Sabbatarianism had been successfully eradicated, but two decades later it reemerged with new vigor. Again the Calvinist authorities suppressed it, and again the Calvinists made many forced converts. As a result of these two suppressions and the conversions that accompanied them, Calvinism became the dominant religion in many towns that previously had been governed by Unitarians, and many of their churches and schools passed into Calvinist hands. As for the Sabbatarians, they managed to survive in the face of oppression for another two and a half centuries by leading a more or less secretive existence. When in 1867 the Hungarian diet decreed the emancipation of Jews, the members of the last congregation, located in a remote mountain village, openly embraced Judaism.

After the formal expulsion of Sabbatarians from their midst, the Unitarian churches enjoyed a period of relative tranquility. It ended, however, in 1629 when a malcontent minister, Mattias Ráv, made a secret visit to Poland to attend the Socinians' general synod. As minister of the Saxon Unitarian church in Kolozsvár, he had twice sought the Unitarian superintendency and the pulpit of the great church in the city, only to be rejected; moreover, he was in trouble with his congregation because of his poor management of church affairs. At the Socinian synod he reported that the Transylvanian Unitarians were in trouble, suffering from weak administrative leadership and lax discipline. The Socinians, accepting his report at face value, responded by sending a letter to their coreligionists in Kolozsvár expressing their concern, offering their support, and suggesting an annual exchange of letters and visits. Ráv's colleagues were understandably upset by the letter, considering his actions to have been highly unethical.

In 1636, when the superintendency was again open, Ráv, who by then had been relieved of his pastorate, sought the position for a third time. Not surprisingly, given the hostility he had generated, he again failed to be chosen, whereupon he challenged the legality of the election. For nearly a year the confirmation of the successful candidate, Daniel Beke, was held up along with his appointment as minister of the great church. Ráv then gathered a group of supporters in the church, and together they brought charges to the prince that the Unitarians were innovators and Beke an apostate and heretic. The prince, a Calvinist, responded by asking for a statement of the Unitarians' belief about Christ and initiating an investigation of his own.

There followed a series of meetings of both the diet and synods, culminating in a special diet held at Deés in 1637. It was a critical time for the Unitarian faith, for its very existence again was threatened. After Ráv and his followers had presented their case for innovation, Beke defended the churches by presenting a new confession of their faith, plus the statement that the ministers had been required to sign in 1579 at Biandrata's insistence following Dávid's imprisonment. The diet deliberated for seven days, with the discussion finally narrowed down to the question of the worship of Christ.

In the end a detailed settlement was agreed to by all parties. Known as the Accord of Deés, the Unitarians agreed to worship and invoke Christ, this to close the door to Sabbatarianism; to practice infant baptism, this in the name of the Father, Son, and Holy Spirit; to celebrate the Lord's Supper; to submit all writings to the prince for approval prior to publication; and to honor their new confession of faith and rules of discipline. Moreover, any Unitarian deemed in violation of the Accord or introducing any innovation would be tried, not by an ecclesiastical synod, but by the civil government. The Accord, voted by the diet with the force of law, was duly signed by the prince and fifty-seven others, including Ráv and Beke. Incidentally, the term "Unitarian" appears some twenty times in the Accord, marking the first time it had been used so widely.

It is hard to judge how willingly the Unitarians entered into this agreement that so narrowly and rigidly defined their doctrine and practice. They had, however, little alternative if their churches were to survive; had they refused, the diet could well have taken away their status as one of the received religions and outlawed them altogether, just as the Socinians were to be outlawed in Poland twenty years later. Eventually the Accord would be interpreted in a more permissive way, for as a Transylvanian Unitarian leader commented many years later in 1875, "In recent times, more favorable to free investigation, many of our doctrines and articles of faith receive a freer and more complete expression, which formerly on account of circumstances of oppression might not be so clearly expressed." For the time being, however, the Transylvanian Unitarians concentrated their attention on applying their faith to the practical problems of everyday life. Beke, whose election had been confirmed by the diet, went on to acquit himself well as superintendent, while Ráv, restored to his pastorate, submitted himself thereafter to the discipline of the church.

At this time the Unitarian cause suffered not only religious restriction, but political restriction as well. Ever since the time of Dávid, the city of Kolozsvár, the center of their movement, had been exclusively under Unitarian control, but under the Calvinist princes the number of Unitarians in the city had decreased, with a corresponding increase in the Calvinist population. Three of the city's churches had come under Calvinist control, and the great church had barely escaped the same fate. The diet took advantage of the new situation by ordering that twenty-five of the 100 seats on the city council should be awarded to Calvinists and that certain high offices should also be open to them. The Unitarians accepted these changes with seeming good grace, and for the next two decades their churches, under the leadership of Beke, went through a period of internal harmony and growth. In 1655, however, their strength was further eroded when the diet ordered that half of the seats in the Kolozsvár council should be occupied by Calvinists. In that same year a great fire, set by Jesuit arsonists, destroyed several of the Unitarians' churches in the city, as well as many of their homes and schools. For two months thereafter students stood watch to prevent the rest of their buildings from being destroyed.

Much greater destruction was soon to follow. The great war that had devastated Poland and led to the expulsion of the Socinians was to have a destructive effect in Transylvania as well. In 1657, after the war had been raging in Poland for nearly a decade, the Transylvanian prince was persuaded, against the strong objection of the Turkish sultan, to enter on the side of the Swedish invaders. At first the prince's army enjoyed some successes, briefly taking control of Kraków, but when the Swedish forces withdrew, hosts of Cossacks swarming in from the east quickly overwhelmed the Transylvanian army. It was almost entirely wiped out, and the prince himself barely escaped with his life.

The Turkish sultan, angered that the prince had rejected

his advice, demanded that he now resign his position. This the prince refused to do, with the result that Transylvania was soon invaded by the Turks from the east and the Austrians from the west. The whole country was devastated, with Kolozsvár, its richest city, suffering most of all. The losses of the Unitarians were staggering, and no sooner had the fighting stopped when the plague erupted, taking a heavy toll. For two years there was no Unitarian superintendent, no synods were held, and the number of students in the college dropped to nine. It was at this low point that the Socinian refugees from Poland reached the city, where, despite their own great problems, the Unitarians welcomed them warmly. As recounted earlier, a number of Polish-speaking congregations were formed, and in time the Socinians were assimilated into the Unitarian culture.

For a generation following the invasion, Transylvania was in effect a vassal state, its princes mere puppets of the sultan. Fortunately for the Unitarians, new leadership emerged in the person of Boldizsár Koncz, who was chosen as superintendent in 1663 and continued to serve in that position for twenty-one years. The times had taken their toll on the Unitarian cause: membership had dwindled, theological discourse was at a low ebb, and the number of churches, once as high as 500 or 600, had decreased to around 200. During Koncz's tenure, however, a revival took place; annual synods were resumed, discipline and morale restored, the church-related schools strengthened, old churches repaired and new ones constructed.

Then shortly before Koncz's death in 1684, the sultan made a determined effort to push on into Western Europe. His forces reached the walls of Vienna, but there the Christian nations rallied to force them back; thereafter the decline in Turkish power was abrupt. By 1686 the Transylvanian prince had reached an accord with the Austrian Emperor Leopold I whereby Transylvania became a part of Hungary; the accord included, moreover, the specific condition "that the four received religions shall never in any way, at any time, or under any pretext be disturbed in the free practice of their religion, and the old laws shall be held sacred."

If the Unitarians hoped for better times under the emperor's regime, they were soon to be disappointed. Leopold was a staunch Roman Catholic over whom the Jesuits exercised great influence, and his rule over Hungary had been marked by continual persecution of the Protestants; in 1674 he had even sentenced forty-one Protestant ministers to the galleys. Once Transylvania had come under his control, his Jesuit advisors quickly persuaded him to make changes in the accord. When the treaty—or diploma, as it was called—was finalized in 1691, many additions had been introduced that over time gave significant advantages to the Catholics at the expense of the Calvinists, Lutherans, and Unitarians. One such addition gave the Catholics the right to reclaim churches and schools that had belonged to them prior to the Reformation. At first, however, the emperor honored his commitment to religious freedom and permitted the Unitarians, now under the able leadership of a new superintendent, Michael Almási, once again to own a printing press. One was imported from Danzig, Poland, at considerable expense, and for twenty years it served the churches well, principally through publishing textbooks for their schools.

Almási's work suffered a severe blow, however, when yet another major fire erupted in Kolozsvár, this one so severe that two-thirds of the city's buildings were destroyed, including three of the Unitarians' churches and two of their schools. "The rich were reduced to poverty," wrote Earl Morse Wilbur, "and the poor to utter destitution." Appeals for financial help were sent out not only to the other Unitarian churches in Transylvania, but also to Dutch Remonstrants; the responses were generous, and rebuilding commenced.

Hardly had the rebuilding been completed, however, when the Catholics, citing the previously mentioned provision in the diploma, laid claim to the rebuilt great church in the marketplace, the minister's home, a school, and other buildings. Only an impassioned plea to the emperor prevented these demands from being met; it did not, however, deter the Catholics from further attempts at encroachment. Under subsequent rulers, the Catholic clergy pressed their claims so vigorously throughout Transylvania that they were able to seize many Unitarian buildings and endowments, sometimes with no pretense at legality whatsoever. On one occasion at a village near Torda a Catholic mob attempted to seize the church when all the men were away, only to be fought off in the courtyard by the younger women while the older ones prayed within. Nevertheless, many of the attempted takeovers succeeded.

Perhaps the most devastating of these takeovers occurred in Kolozsvár in 1716 when government troops occupied the city, seized the great church and two smaller churches, and plundered the homes of the ministers, teachers, and leading laypeople, seizing many valuable articles, including the printing press. The great church was then reconsecrated and refitted for Catholic worship; two years later the Unitarian college was also seized. Despite many appeals by the Unitarians, none of the property was ever returned, nor was any compensation made. In 1724, at the height of this oppression, Superintendent Almási died, his death undoubtedly hastened by stress. Despite his best efforts, many churches and schools had been lost during his long tenure, and the total membership of the churches had declined to 30,000.

Following Almási's death, the Unitarians, in the face of persistent oppression and with their grievances ignored, withdrew more and more from public life into their own small circles, trying to make themselves as inconspicuous as possible. There was a real danger that their demoralized movement, now stalled, would slowly wither away through attrition and lack of inspirational leadership. Fortunately at this critical point a new leader emerged in the person of Michael Lombard Szentábrahámi who, through his energy and wisdom, was able to bring to the movement new life and direction. It was he who, as a minister and young professor at the Unitarian college at Kolozsvár, had found new quarters for the college after its buildings had been seized and who later, as rector, was largely responsible for its survival. His extensive lectures, circulated in manuscript form before being published posthumously, broke no new ground theologically but helped several generations of Unitarians in the understanding and practice of their faith, while at the same time blunting some of the hostility directed toward them.

In 1737, after completing his tenure as rector, he was elected Unitarian superintendent. A versatile man, Szentábrahámi was an able administrator, a respected scholar, and an inspiring teacher and preacher. Popular and admired, he became known to his contemporaries as "the eye, heart, and tongue of the Unitarians." While competent in all fields, his greatest contributions were in education. As superintendent, he greatly strengthened the churches' schools, thus building a base for Unitarian survival and future growth. By the time of his death in 1758 his work had born such fruit that he was deservedly called "the second founder of the Unitarian Church."

It was indeed fortunate that Szentábrahámi had done his work well, for a new period of oppression had already begun prior to his death. In 1740, Maria Theresia had inherited the throne of the Austrian Empire. While she is honored as one of the great monarchs in European history, she was an unremitting foe of all Protestants, and especially of Unitarians. She had, as had her predecessors, taken the usual oath guaranteeing the rights of the received religions of Transylvania, but when a Unitarian delegation came to pledge their loyalty she refused to give them an audience.

Within a few years she had, with the help of Jesuit advisors, drawn up a plan for the systematic oppression of Unitarianism. The plan started by replacing Unitarians holding public office; then the ministers found themselves faced with numerous legal restrictions. They were prohibited from making converts, from permitting a member of a non-Unitarian church to marry a member of their own, from publicly debating religious questions, from going outside the geographical boundaries of their parishes in performance of pastoral duties, from giving religious instruction to children, from building or repairing churches without royal approval, and from publishing books without royal approval. (Such approval was seldom forthcoming; the publication of only two Unitarian books was permitted during the empress's forty-year reign.)

The Catholics took over some village churches, historically in the hands of a Unitarian majority, by engineering an influx of enough Catholics to shift the balance; in other villages, Catholics would instigate disturbances so that the Unitarians could be penalized for disturbing the peace. Finally, a strong effort was made to convert Unitarians to Catholicism: in Kolozsvár the Unitarian schools were closed and the children required to attend Catholic ones; in other places children sometimes were enrolled in Catholic schools after being removed forcefully from their homes; those wishing to attend Protestant universities in other countries were denied passports and encouraged to go to the Catholic university in Vienna instead; political inducements were offered to the Unitarian nobility to make them change their faith. This last tactic was in fact so successful that by the end of Maria Theresia's reign in 1780 the Unitarian churches had become predominantly ones of the middle and lower classes, and the overall plan had succeeded in winning several thousand converts to Catholicism.

In the final years of her reign Maria Theresia, influenced by her son Joseph, softened her position and in time expelled the Jesuits from her land. Thereafter, the persecution of the Unitarians lessened, and with her death in 1780 and the accession of Joseph to the throne, the Unitarians could at last begin building on the foundation that Szentábrahámi had laid. Already as prince, Joseph had come to Kolozsvár to hear the Unitarians' complaints, and there he had given them an indication of better things to come: "We say," stated the prince, "that nobody finds salvation outside of the faith of Rome, but it would not be wrong to allow the possibility for everybody to choose that particular way to heaven which he [or she] likes."

The reign of Joseph (as Emperor Joseph II) marked a turning point in the fortunes of the Transylvanian Unitarians. He and his successors were fair-minded, liberal rulers who promoted the religious freedom and toleration that the Unitarians sorely needed after almost two centuries of oppression. Leopold II, Joseph's brother who succeeded him in 1790, restored to them their right to a fair share of public offices and hence became known as "the restorer of the rights of Unitarians." During this period the Unitarians' renaissance was ably led by their superintendents, Stephen Agh and Stephen Lázár. In 1785, Agh received permission to publish Szentábrahámi's writings, generally referred to collectively as simply the *Summa*; these were widely circulated throughout Western Europe, promoting a deeper and more positive understanding of Unitarianism. Lázár, who served from 1786 until 1811, was particularly effective in raising morale in the churches and in gaining the support of the Transylvanian nobility.

The cause was further aided by a substantial bequest from a prominent layman, Ladislas Suki, who died in 1792. He was the last surviving member of an old noble family and had been a loyal church supporter throughout his life. As a result of his bequest it became possible to increase the salaries of the superintendent and the professors; to give financial aid to poor ministers, their widows, and students; and to establish a permanent Unitarian endowment fund. With additional gifts supplementing Suki's bequest, the Unitarians in Kolozsvár were able to erect a fine new church, which is still in use (they had been worshiping in a private home after their former church had been confiscated by the Catholics), plus a new college building and homes for the superintendent and professors. In 1827 another large gift was received, this from Pál Augusztinovics of the royal Austrian court and a descendant of Socinian exiles who had come to Transylvania in 1660. Son of a Unitarian minister, both he and his mother had been aided by the Suki fund following his father's death. At his own death in 1837 he left the bulk of his estate to the Unitarian Church, making his total contributions greater than its entire previous assets.

With a strong financial base, able leadership, and a new freedom from oppression, the Transylvanian Unitarians enjoyed steady growth throughout the first half of the nineteenth century. The number of churches grew to over 100, and total membership approached 50,000. It was during this period that the Transylvanian and British Unitarians discovered each other's existence, with each group thrilled to find another bearing the same name. They established ties that have continued to the present day. Soon afterward, ties were likewise established between the Transylvanian and American Unitarians; these, too, have persisted.

In the mid-nineteenth century the period of peace and growth came temporarily to an end. The Hungarians had long resented Austrian rule, and in 1848 they revolted, declared their independence, and formed a national government at Budapest. Later that same year a union between Hungary and Transylvania was established, and Unitarianism became recognized as one of the official "received" religions throughout the entire land. One of the leaders of the revolution was János Pálfy, a Transylvanian Unitarian who was elected vice president of the united parliament. The new government proved to be short-lived, however, for the Austrian emperor enlisted the help of the Russian czar, and together with great cruelty they put down the revolution. Romanian peasants who had long suffered under their Hungarian masters used the occasion to wreak revenge, with many men, women, and children slaughtered and whole villages wiped out; the Unitarians, like all Hungarians, suffered heavy losses of both life and property. Pálfy was among those sentenced to death for his part in the revolution, but he eventually was pardoned and lived to write an account of the uprising.

Once back in control, the Austrian government attempted to permanently weaken the Protestants, especially the Unitarians, by imposing new regulations on their schools. Under the pretense of strengthening the educational system, the government imposed a salary scale for teachers that the Unitarians found impossible to meet. Fortunately, however, before the government could take control of the Unitarian schools and introduce a Catholic curriculum, the British Unitarians raised enough money to satisfy the salary requirements. The money was delivered in person by the secretary of the British and Foreign Unitarian Association, who with his daughter came to Kolozsvár in 1858, the first British Unitarians to visit their Transylvanian counterparts. The American Unitarians had planned to help as well, but a national financial panic thwarted their effort.

In the end, this attempt to weaken the Protestants not only failed, it also had some important positive effects for the Unitarian cause. A new and lasting spirit of cooperation had been established between the Unitarians, Calvinists, and Lutherans of Transylvania, with old hostilities overcome as they united in a common cause. In addition, the ties of the Transylvanian Unitarians to their coreligionists in England and America had been strengthened, with several positive results. The major writings of the American Unitarian William Ellery Channing were translated and published in Hungarian, and Transylvanian students began visiting the Unitarian colleges at Oxford, London, and Manchester. English and American visitors started coming to ceremonial occasions in Transylvania: the three-hundredth anniversary of the proclamation of religious freedom in 1868, the three-hundredth anniversary of Dávid's death in 1879, the opening of a new college building in Kolozsvár in 1901, and the four-hundredth anniversary of Dávid's birth in 1910.

By 1861, Austrian suppression had relaxed to the point that the Unitarians were permitted to convene a synod for the purpose of electing a leader. Their choice was János Kriza, well known as a writer, poet, minister, and professor at the college in Kolozsvár; he was given the title of "bishop," by then considered more appropriate than "superintendent." It was under his able leadership that Transylvanian Unitarianism underwent a revitalization; ties with the British and American Unitarians were strengthened, rural congregations and their schools were rejuvenated, and a theological journal, *Keresztény Magvető*, was established which is still being published. During his tenure the Austrian government began a partial subsidization of the Unitarian churches and their schools at the same level as those of the other denominations, a practice that was to continue until the end of the Second World War.

After Kriza's death in 1876, József Ferencz, a young minister and professor at Kolozsvár, was elected as his successor; he was to serve as bishop for the next fifty-two years! Ferencz had preached the first public Unitarian sermon in Budapest on June 13, 1869, an event still celebrated each year in that city. It was during his tenure that not only the Budapest church but several others were established in that part of Hungary lying outside of Transylvania, the first Unitarian churches in that region for over a century. In fact, Budapest was soon to become an important center of Hungarian Unitarianism, second only to Kolozsvár; in 1896 it was the site of an International Conference of Unitarians.

Twelve years earlier Unitarianism had been further strengthened when a layman, Mózes Berde, willed all his property to the Unitarian Church with the following declaration: "I had been struggling for a saving purpose all my life. I wanted to show that even a poor man with a strong will can be of use to society, humanity, and the nation. . . . From my youth one sentiment has been nurtured in my heart, one thought in my mind: to help my poor religious community to rise, to make it easier for students to master the sciences, and to give relief to its old servants and professors." It was another example of the deep loyalty that the Unitarian faith had engendered.

By the end of the nineteenth century, the Hungarian Unitarian Church, as it was now called, found itself in a strong condition. Its constituency had grown to over 75,000, and it could boast more than 160 congregations, forty-two intermediate schools, three academies, a college that included a theological school, and a new headquarters under construction in Kolozsvár. It enjoyed religious freedom, held equal status with other faiths, had had a succession of able leaders, was well financed, and was becoming part of an international Unitarian community. Its perseverance through almost two centuries of oppression and persecution had proved well worth the cost.

The Beginnings of Unitarianism in England

The history of English Unitarianism is less known than it deserves to be. Many of its passages being obscure, and the threads of its story being complicated, it has not presented itself as an easy study. . . . Yet the history of the Unitarian movement is the key to its meaning.

—ALEXANDER GORDON, 1895

*O*n April 17, 1774, the first avowedly Unitarian congregation in England gathered for worship for the first time. By then it had been over a century since the Socinian churches in Poland had been forced out of existence and two centuries since the Unitarian churches in Transylvania had had their freedom restricted by the innovation law; thus each of these three essentially homegrown movements can be seen as having its unique time line. It is true that for well over 200 years there had been outbreaks of Arian, Socinian, and Unitarian thought in England, but no organized, lasting movement had resulted until Theophilus Lindsey, with the help of his wife Hannah and a few friends, rented an auction hall on Essex Street in London, fitted it as a chapel, and opened its doors for worship. Although that first service had been advertised only by word of mouth, some 200 people were in attendance, most of them dissatisfied members of the Church of England (also known as the Anglican Church). Among those present was Benjamin Franklin, then in London to exert his influence on behalf of the American colonies. Lindsey, who had just left the Anglican ministry, led the service using an unconventional liturgy and without wearing the customary clerical vestment.

His sermon dealt with the need for a harmonious spirit in religion, and he pledged to avoid controversial subjects in his sermons, a pledge that he later would find hard to honor.

Theophilus Lindsey was fifty-one, his wife Hannah thirty-four, when they arrived in London to start their bold venture. He had served most of his adult life as a clergyman in the Church of England but had become progressively uncomfortable with its theology. His study of the Bible forced him first to an Arian, then to a fully Unitarian position, which made it impossible for him to continue leading Anglican worship without sacrificing his own integrity. Many of his colleagues had secretly come to similar conclusions but stayed on in their positions; nevertheless, when they learned that Lindsey planned to resign, all were shocked and some offended. They first attempted to persuade him to change his mind, then to discredit him. They even promised Hannah a comfortable home if she would leave her husband, but she indignantly refused the offer.

Lindsey's parishioners in Catterick were grief-stricken by his decision, for he had been an extremely dedicated, caring minister whom they deeply loved. In late 1773, after bidding sad farewells, the couple set out for London with hardly any money, but with a firm conviction that they were doing what their conscience required of them. With the help of friends they rented a modest apartment and the hall in Essex Street and opened the makeshift chapel for worship. The congregation prospered from the start, and within three years they purchased and remodeled the Essex Street property to provide a large chapel above and living quarters below. The time, it seems, was ripe for just such an innovative institutional expression of Christian faith. (It is of interest that only a short while earlier the first avowedly Universalist congregation in England had emerged, also in London, under the leadership of James Relly.)

For a quarter of a century there had been clear signs of unrest among the Anglican clergy. Each minister at ordination or on elevation to a higher office long had been required to subscribe to "all and every Articles [of faith] as agreeable to the Word of God," referring to the Anglican creedal statement called the Thirty-Nine Articles. In addition, before heading a parish each had to promise, "I do declare that I will conform to the Liturgy of the Church of England as it is now by law established." The liturgy, contained in the church's Book of Common Prayer, included the Athanasian Creed and other elements that, by the middle of the century, many of the clergy considered to be outmoded and in need of revision.

The matter had come to a head in 1749 with the publication of an anonymous work entitled *Free and Candid Disquisitions relating to the Church of England.* Quite moderate in tone and content, it proposed simply a new translation of the Bible and some changes in the liturgy; it nevertheless had prompted lively debate and a variety of reactions. The Anglican bishops had united in defending the *status quo* and to varying degrees attempted to force conformity, hence the term "nonconformist" for those not following Anglican standards of faith and practice. At least one parish minister had been formally reprimanded for omitting the creed from the liturgy; others would have the parish clerk read those portions of the liturgy to which they could not in good conscience subscribe. Another showed his disrespect for the creed by having it sung to the tune of a popular hunting song, while yet another introduced its reading by saying, "Brethren, this is the Creed of St. Athanasius, but God forbid it should be the creed of any other man."

Only one minister, William Robertson, who served an Irish parish, had taken the honorable step of resigning once the issue had been raised and he found himself no longer able to honor his vows. His act of conscience cost him dearly in terms of worldly wealth; a married man with twenty-one children, he spent the rest of his life in poverty as a poorly paid schoolteacher. However, his act of courage inspired Lindsey to do likewise a decade later and earned for him from Lindsey the title of "father of Unitarian nonconformity."

In 1771 a group of reform-minded Anglicans had gathered in London, organized the Feathers Tavern Association (named after their meeting place), and twice petitioned Parliament for the abolition of the subscription requirement for clergy. Their second petition offered the following declaration as a substitute for subscription to the Thirty-Nine Articles: "We declare, as in the presence of Almighty God, that we believe that the Holy Scriptures of the Old and New Testaments contain a revelation of the mind and will of God, and that we receive them as the Rule of our Faith and practice." Parliament rejected this second petition, as they had the first; a similar petition, made to the bishops, had suffered the same fate. Of the more than 200 clergymen who signed the petition, the vast majority stayed where they were; only a half dozen withdrew from their ministries. Among that half dozen was Theophilus Lindsey.

As mentioned previously, there had been numerous expressions of antitrinitarian views in Britain long before the organization of the Unitarian chapel in Essex Street. The road to that chapel was, historically speaking, a long and winding one with many branches; or to invoke a different metaphor suggested by Jeremy Goring, the early history of English Unitarianism, rather than following a stream, is more "a series of unconnected whirlpools." As elsewhere in Western Europe, the widespread availability of the Bible, which first took place during the sixteenth century, and the subsequent great diversity of interpretations, made such views almost inevitable. As Earl Morse Wilbur has commented, the "independent study of the Bible must be regarded as the most fundamental of all the influences that combined in shaping the Unitarian movement." And it must be remembered that Socinianism throughout its history and Unitarianism (as well as Universalism) until relatively recent times were essentially Bible-based religions. Thus in England, John Wycliffe's translation of the Bible into English in the late fourteenth century had sown the seeds for the growth of liberal, heretical thought.

The religious situation in the country during the sixteenth century underwent dramatic fluctuations, influenced in large part by those who occupied the throne. The long reign of Henry VIII (1509-47), the short reigns of Edward VI (1547-53) and Mary I (1553-58), and the long reign of Elizabeth I (1558-1603) each brought substantial change. Henry, by declaring his country's independence from papal authority and establishing the Church of England in 1534, not only started the English Reformation, but at the same time opened it as a haven to those suffering persecution on the Continent. In fact, during the next year a host of Anabaptists, many with Arian views, crossed the English Channel and settled in the eastern counties. As a result, Henry ordered Archbishop Thomas Cranmer to identify and prosecute those who denied the Trinity, and fourteen were burned as heretics; nevertheless, many went unpunished, and Arianism continued to be professed more or less openly.

During Edward's reign, with the number of religious refugees continuing to rise, Cranmer led a stronger effort to stop the spread of Arianism. Several of those found guilty of the heresy recanted, but one prominent Flemish physician, Dr. George van Parris, did not. Tried before Cranmer through an interpreter (van Parris spoke no English), he declared "that he believeth that God the Father is the only God, and that Christ is not very God." Refusing to renounce his views, he was burned at the stake at Smithfield in 1551, two years before Michael Servetus was to meet a similar fate at Geneva.

The archbishop, as part of his program to strengthen the Church of England, also sought out those in the clergy suspected of holding unsound doctrine. John Assheton, priest of Shiltelington, was found guilty of maintaining "that the trinitie of persons was established by the confession [creed] of Athanasius . . . and that the hollie Ghoste is not God, but only a certeyn power of the Father; secundarilye, that Jesus Christ, that was cionceived of the virgyn Mary, was a holy prophet and speciallie beloved of God the Father, but that he was not the true and lyving God." Facing death at the stake, Assheton renounced these "errors, heresies, and damnable opinions" and thus his life was spared. He was the first member of the established clergy to be arraigned on antitrinitarian charges, though not the last. Cranmer, in a further effort to strengthen the church, also invited distinguished Protestant scholars from the Continent to teach at English universities; among those invited were Bernardino Ochino and Laelius Socinus, whose views were not yet suspect.

A violent reaction to the Reformation occurred during the reign of Mary, an ardent and uncompromising Roman Catholic. Nearly 300 Protestants, including Cranmer, were put to death; another 800 fled the country. The Strangers' (i.e., foreigners) Church, which had been established in London to accommodate refugees and visitors, was closed down. Laws favoring the Protestants were repealed and old Catholic laws revived. Those of the lower or humble classes were not immune from persecution; for example, one Patrick Packingham, a dealer in hides, was burned as an Arian even though he recanted at the stake. Passions over religious views ran high, even in prison. A clergyman, jailed for his Protestant views, became so incensed during an argument with a fellow prisoner, jailed for his Arian views, that he spit in the Arian's face. Later, he justified his action by publishing a tract with the following title: "An Apology of John Philpot; written for spitting upon an Arian: with an invective against Arians, the veri natural children of Antichrist: with an admonition to all that be faithful in Christ, to beware of them, and of other late sprung heresies, as of the most enemies of the gospel." Philpot was sent to the stake in 1555; what happened to the Arian is not recorded.

With Mary's death in 1558 and Elizabeth's accession to the throne, Protestantism was quickly restored. The new queen was anxious to unite her people by making the Church of England a truly national institution, built around beliefs and practices acceptable to the overwhelming majority. Accordingly, its doctrine was a compromise between Calvin and Luther, its liturgy a blend of Protestant and Catholic. By an Act of Uniformity all persons, clergy and laity alike, were required to attend the religious services sanctioned by law, with a fine of one shilling for each absence. The Strangers' Church was reopened and laws for the burning of heretics repealed. It soon became obvious, however, that many heresies had survived Mary's bloodbath and still remained in the land. One bishop, on returning from exile in Germany, wrote a friend: "We found at the beginning of the reign of Elizabeth a large and inauspicious crop of Arians, Anabaptists, and other pests, which I know not how, but as mushrooms spring up in the night and in darkness, so these sprung up in that darkness and unhappy night of the Marian times."

To cope with this problem, in 1560 all Anabaptists were ordered to leave the country since they refused to attend services at either the national church or the Strangers' Church. The order was for the most part ignored, with the Anabaptists worshiping together in secret; their numbers, in fact, were increasing. On Easter Sunday, 1575, the authorities surprised a small group worshiping in a London home and imprisoned twenty-five of them. The following month, five recanted and agreed to attend services; they were forced to stand in St. Paul's churchyard "with a fagot [a bundle of twigs] tied on their shoulders, as a token that they were worthy of burning" while the bishop preached a sermon. The rest, refusing to recant, were condemned to death as heretics, although the sentences of fourteen women and a youth were later commuted; they were taken by ship to Holland. Of the others, one died in prison, two were burned at the stake, and two were eventually released. The two who were executed were judged to have particularly heretical views regarding the doctrine of the incarnation—that God had become incarnate in the person of Jesus. They "died in great horror, with crying and roaring." Unlike some who were burnt, their deaths were not hastened by preliminary suffocation or strangulation or by the explosion of a sack of gunpowder tied around the neck. The queen excused the executions on the grounds that, since she had recently approved capital punishment for traitors to the state, she could do no less for those who had dishonored God. By the end of her reign in 1603, however, the heresy fires had stopped burning, to be relit only briefly by her successor.

The seventeenth century in England was marked by a decline in the power of the monarchy and a corresponding increase in the power of Parliament, a shift necessarily affecting the religious climate. Since Elizabeth, "the Virgin Queen," had no heir, the crown passed at her death from the House of Tudor to the House of Stuart, with James VI of Scotland becoming James I of England as well. Bred a strict Calvinist, he reigned from 1603 to 1625, and was succeeded by his son, Charles I, whose inability to work with Parliament eventually cost him his life. After he was beheaded in 1649, England became for a decade a Puritan commonwealth led first by Parliament and then, after 1653, by Oliver Cromwell, who as "protector" (as he was called), favored religious freedom, at least in theory.

As the seventeenth century began, however, James I asserted his supreme ecclesiastical authority as "Defender of the Faith" over all religious matters. (Since the break with the Roman church some seventy years before, English monarchs had been head of both church and state). He attempted to stamp out heresy, whether domestic or imported from abroad. Two more burnings for heresy took place, the last to be carried out in England; the practice was discontinued because of its ineffectiveness as a deterrent and because the public had come to sympathize with the victims rather than to abhor their views. An historian reported that the king "politicly preferred that heretics hereafter, though condemned, should silently and privately waste themselves away in the prison rather than to grace them, and amuse others, with the solemnity of public execution, which in popular judgments usurped the honor of the persecution."

An attempt, largely unsuccessful, was made to stop the flow of Socinian materials coming into the country from the Raków press in Poland by way of Holland. When James learned that a Latin edition of the *Racovian Catechism* had been dedicated to him by the translator, he ordered all copies to be burnt in public. In the later years of his reign the king gave less attention to doctrinal matters, instead devoting his energy to preserving the episcopal structure of the Anglican Church under which the bishops came to office through royal appointment. He was an adamant foe of the Puritans, members of a movement that originally arose within the Church of England, so-called because they were striving for a "purer" church, rid of all remaining Roman Catholic elements. "I will make them conform themselves," he threatened, "or I will harry them out of the land, or else do worse."

James I was unable to make good his threat. During the reign of his son, Charles I, which began in 1625, the Puritans pushed their cause with increasing vigor, demanding a presbyterian form of church government with the leadership chosen by the ministers themselves, rather than the hierarchical structure of the Anglican Church. They also had a strong commitment to strict purity of doctrine, culminating in the adoption of the Westminster Confession of Faith in 1649, the same year in which Parliament found the king guilty of treason and had him beheaded. The Confession replaced, at least temporarily, the Thirty-Nine Articles as the doctrinal standard of the Church of England.

The preceding year the Presbyterians, as one group of Puritans was now called, had secured passage of "An Ordinance of the Lords and Commons assembled in Parliament for punishing Blasphemies and Heresies." Popularly known as the "Draconic Ordinance," it provided that "all persons that willingly, by preaching, teaching, printing, or writing, maintain and publish that the Father is not God, the Son is not God, or that the Holy Ghost is not God, or that they three are not one eternal God, or that Christ is not God equal with the

Father [besides seven other named heresies], shall be adjudged guilty of felony; and in case the party upon his trial shall not adjure his said error he shall suffer the pains of death, without benefit of clergy." It then listed sixteen other less serious crimes for which the penalty was merely imprisonment. It was to be the last in a series of attempts by the Presbyterians to suppress religious freedom. Only seven months later a second group of Puritans, the Independents, succeeded in having the Presbyterian members forcefully ejected from Parliament by a group of soldiers led by one of Oliver Cromwell's officers, Colonel Pride; "Pride's Purge" it was called.

It was indeed fortunate for the Unitarian cause that the "Draconic Ordinance" was never enforced, for in 1647, John Biddle, a young schoolmaster, had published a tract entitled *XII Arguments drawn out of the Scripture* in which he carefully refuted on logical grounds the traditional doctrine of the Holy Spirit. An excellent teacher and scholar with an independent turn of mind, he knew most of the New Testament by heart and had concluded, quite without the influence of Socinian writings, that the doctrine of the Trinity was both unscriptural and unreasonable. His *XII Arguments* had been written in 1644 for circulation only among close friends, but when the authorities learned of its existence they first put him in jail, then placed him under house arrest for the next three years while attempts were made to dissuade him from his heretical views. Among those who attempted to dissuade him was Archbishop Usher, the same church leader who had calculated the date of creation as 4004 BCE.

Impatient to have his case settled, Biddle then forced the issue by having his tract printed and publicly distributed. Its publication caused an immediate sensation; copies were confiscated and burnt by the hangman, but the demand was so great that a second edition soon appeared. Biddle himself was sent back to prison. Some demanded his death, but uncowed and confident, he published while in captivity two additional and more comprehensive works, including *A Confession of*

Faith Touching the Holy Trinity. In his *Confession* he presented an unorthodox view of the doctrine, including his conviction that Jesus "hath no other than a human nature," thereby prompting vigorous attempts at refutation.

Biddle was to spend the rest of his life in and out of prison as the political power in the country continued to shift. When Oliver Cromwell became protector in 1653, he secured passage by Parliament of an Act of Oblivion whereby, with few exceptions, all those accused of any crime were set free. Biddle's freedom was to be short-lived, however, for he soon published a catechism that was judged heretical, standing as it did in marked contrast to the newly adopted Westminster Catechism. Not only did it reject the Trinity and the deity of Christ, but it also described God in crudely anthropomorphic terms—in this he seems to have surpassed even Archbishop Usher in a strictly literal interpretation of the Bible!

Again Biddle was imprisoned, his catechism was burnt, and fresh demands were made that he be executed. However, in the confused religious climate then existing, after only six months the charges against him were dropped. Once more his freedom was short-lived, for after he began holding meetings with his followers new charges were filed against him as a blasphemer. Cromwell, who had promised religious freedom under the protectorate, reluctantly succumbed to the advocates of doctrinal soundness and banished Biddle to the Scilly Islands (an archipelago southwest of England) for life imprisonment. Cromwell did, however, grant his prisoner an annual subsidy of a hundred crowns for subsistence. Not long before Cromwell's death, Biddle again was released to rejoin his followers, but they soon were forced to conduct their meetings in secret when the ban on nonconformist worship was reinstituted on the restoration of the monarchy in 1660.

In 1662, despite their attempts at secrecy, Biddle and a group of friends were surprised and arrested while holding a worship service in a private residence. Unable to pay his fine, Biddle once again was sent to prison, where he soon became gravely ill. Two days after his release, he died, being then in his forty-seventh year. His little group of followers, without a leader and in constant danger of arrest, did not long survive him. Nevertheless, for his persistence, influence, and his courageous and open exposition of beliefs, John Biddle has long been known as "the father of English Unitarians," even though others might properly share the title.

A few months prior to Biddle's death a bigoted, anti-Puritan Parliament, reacting strongly to Cromwell's policies, passed an Act of Uniformity that placed even greater restrictions on nonconformists. It required every clergyman to give unqualified assent to the entire contents of the Book of Common Prayer and to preach and conduct worship in strict compliance with its provisions. The vast majority of the nonconforming clergy, well over 2,000 in number, refused to comply. They thus were ejected from their pulpits and "went out not knowing whither they went." Three years later the infamous Five Mile Act was passed, forbidding any ejected minister from coming within five miles of any city or town in which he had served. The Great Ejection, as it came to be known, brought great suffering to many and the seeds sown by the heroic protest of the Dissenters (as the nonconformists had begun to be called) were to germinate only slowly. However, as one British historian has stated, "the real beginning of the Churches which developed later into what is generally known as Unitarian or free Christian took place in 1662, when two thousand ministers refused to accept the Act of Uniformity."

Following Biddle's death there followed a lapse of some twenty-five years before new leaders emerged to promote Unitarian views in England. Nevertheless, Socinian books continued to pour into the country unhindered by the authorities. As one member of Parliament complained, "There is a very great neglect somewhere, wheresoever the inspection of books is lodged, that at least the *Socinian* books are tolerated, and sell as openly as the Bible." Thus heretical views were quietly spreading throughout the country, influencing the thought of such intellectual leaders as John Milton and Sir Isaac Newton, both of whom came privately to antitrinitarian positions.

Following Cromwell's death in 1658, his son Richard, as successor, was able to retain power for only another two years. Accordingly, the monarchy was restored in 1660, with Charles II, son of the ill-fated Charles I, put on the throne; he reigned for the next twenty-five years. Though a "closet" Catholic, he worked closely with the anti-Puritan Parliament to stamp out nonconformity and to strengthen the established church. His son, James II, who was openly Catholic, aroused so much hostility because of his religion that after only three years he was forced to flee to France. His wife had just borne a son, and the Protestants of the established Church of England, fearful of a Catholic succession, engineered a bloodless revolution that placed William III and Mary II, daughter of James II by an earlier marriage, on the throne as co-rulers. Mary died in 1694, leaving her husband to reign alone until his death in 1702. The revolution also produced a Bill of Rights that forever excluded Roman Catholics from the English throne.

With the death of Charles II the religious climate had begun to change, and in 1689, following the short and stormy reign of James II, Parliament passed the Act of Toleration, making it again lawful for nonconformists, other than Catholics and deniers of the Trinity, to hold public worship. (Unitarians were not given full freedom under the law until 1813.) Then a few months later Stephen Nye, with the help of two of Biddle's disciples, Thomas Firmin and Henry Hedworth, published anonymously *A Brief History of the Unitarians, called also Socinians.* It marked the first time that the word "Unitarian" had appeared in print in England, some ninety years after it first had appeared in Transylvania. A series of *Unitarian Tracts* by Nye, again published anonymously, followed over the next few years, vigorously promoting the Unitarian point of view.

Predictably, these tracts drew sharp responses; they also precipitated a decade-long controversy within the Church of

England, popularly known as "The Trinitarian Controversy," which arose when some eminent Oxford divines sought to simplify and make more intelligible the doctrine of the Trinity. However, their attempt led to such divisiveness that the university finally ordered the end of any further discussion of the subject, but the controversy apparently did lead to some greater degree of tolerance within the Anglican Church. The cause of toleration also was furthered during this period by the writings of the great philosopher John Locke, known as "the father of English Rationalism"; his *Letter on Toleration* became a landmark in the history of religious freedom, and his *Reasonableness of Christianity as delivered in Scriptures* did much to promote the Unitarian cause.

The eighteenth century was marked by doctrinal turmoil both within the Church of England and among the Dissenters as both parties struggled with issues of tolerance and with the role of reason in the interpretation of scripture. No longer did the monarchy play a significant part in determining the religious climate; its former dominating power was gone forever and henceforth the major players would be the clergy, the theologians, and the Parliament.

Hardly had the new century begun when another theological controversy broke out within the established church, this one over the doctrine of the person of Christ. A movement had arisen at Cambridge to restore the faith and practice of the Church to that of "primitive Christianity," a consequence of which was the formulation of a basically Arian Christology. The leading spokesperson for this "Arian movement" was Samuel Clarke, a highly respected member of the clergy who served both as rector of an important parish and as chaplain to the queen. Regarded as the Anglican Church's leading theologian, it was widely believed that he would in time become Archbishop of Canterbury, the highest-ranking office in the Church of England. Harboring secret doubts about the Trinity, he had made an exhaustive study of the New Testament in an attempt to come to a better understanding of the doctrine.

In 1712 he published his conclusions in *The Scripture-doctrine of the Trinity*, based on a careful evaluation of 1,251 relevant Bible passages. Clarke concluded that the Father alone is the supreme God; that the Son, though eternal, is a subordinate being, worthy of worship on a lower level; and that the Holy Spirit is also a subordinate being, for whom scripture offers no basis for worship; considered together, these three constitute the Trinity.

The conservatives in the Anglican Church considered Clarke's views to be Arian heresy and brought his case to Parliament. Clarke at this point made a partial retraction and no official action against him was taken; thereafter his influence declined and he was dismissed from the queen's chaplaincy. (Sixty years later Theophilus Lindsey's Essex Street Chapel adopted many of the revisions that Clarke had vainly proposed for the Book of Common Prayer; in fact, it was not until 1928 that the use of the Athanasian Creed was made optional in the Church of England.) Although his efforts to reform official Anglican theology failed, Clarke's viewpoint nevertheless did find some acceptance within the church; as a result, a significant number of the clergy began resorting to what became notorious as the "Arian Subscription" by publicly subscribing to the Church of England's articles of faith while privately holding Arian or other heretical beliefs. It was among the Dissenters, however, that the Arian movement was to make its greatest impact.

Thomas Emlyn, a Presbyterian minister in Dublin, Ireland, was undoubtedly the most influential of the Arian Dissenters during this period. A beloved pastor and preacher, he was nevertheless suspected of heresy by a conservative parishioner who noticed that he avoided any mention of the Trinity. Attacked by ministerial colleagues after admitting that he believed in the supreme deity of only God the Father, Emlyn in 1702 published a tract entitled *An Humble Inquiry into the Scripture Account of Jesus Christ* in which he explained and defended his position. Two of the most intolerant Dissenters then had him arrested on charges of blasphemy. A jury found him guilty "of writing and publishing an infamous and scandalous libel declaring that Jesus Christ is not the supreme God," and a civil judge sentenced him to a year in prison plus a heavy fine. As one sympathetic bishop said of the case, "The Non-conformists accused him, the Conformists condemned him, the Secular power was called in, and the cause ended in an imprisonment and a very great fine: two methods of conviction about which the gospel is silent."

Emlyn remained in prison for more than two years, unable to pay the fine levied against him but preaching on Sundays to his fellow prisoners and members of his former congregation who came to hear him. (That congregation, incidentally, in time moved first to an Arian, then to a Unitarian position.) Emlyn's case aroused much interest and sympathy; he was, in fact, the last Dissenter to be imprisoned for denying the Trinity. After finally obtaining his release, he moved from Dublin to London, where he became a close friend of Samuel Clarke. His *Humble Inquiry* and subsequent writings did much to move the liberal wing of the Dissenters toward an Arian position.

Meanwhile the Dissenters had taken on new vitality following the passage of the Act of Toleration and began moving their worship from private homes into the new "chapels" they were erecting. (The term "church" was reserved by the Church of England for its own use.) Their ranks were made up for the most part of Presbyterians, Baptists, and Independents. Of these the Independents, as strict Calvinists, were the most conservative and at the same time the most democratic; the Presbyterians, drifting steadily away from a strict Calvinist theology, were not only the most numerous, but also the most wealthy; while the Baptists, largely from the humbler classes, were the most tolerant with regard to doctrine. In the new atmosphere of freedom it was inevitable that more and more differences of doctrinal opinion would emerge within the Dissenters' ranks, and it was not long before such differences led to serious divisions. In 1717 a controversy arose at

Exeter in southwestern England among the nonconformist congregations; it resulted in the dismissal of two ministers on grounds of Arianism. Their followers quickly organized a new congregation, and on the Sunday following the dismissal they opened a new place of worship. The first congregation in England to be avowedly antitrinitarian, it has survived to the present day. The controversy brought much public attention to the beliefs of the two dismissed ministers, much of it favorable; thereafter antitrinitarianism flourished in that section of England.

The controversy at Exeter was followed almost at once by the so-called Salters' Hall Controversy, named after the place in London at which it occurred. A leader of the Dissenting party in Parliament, in an attempt to keep the Dissenters united as a political force, had drawn up a manifesto designed to prevent the kind of divisiveness that was being experienced at Exeter. The manifesto, known as "Advices for Peace," sought to confine the settlement of doctrinal differences to the congregation in which they had occurred and suggested ways in which this might be accomplished. To gain support for this manifesto, a meeting of all the Dissenting ministers in London was called for February 19, 1719, in Salters' Hall. Apparently over 200 attended that first meeting; of the 150 subsequently identified in the accounts, 80 were Presbyterians, 40 Independents, and 30 Baptists.

The originator of the manifesto had hoped to confine discussion to its contents, with no discussion whatsoever of doctrinal matters, but almost at once one of the conservative Independent ministers moved that the "Advices," which were to be put to their first use at Exeter, be accompanied by a declaration of faith in the doctrine of the Trinity. A bitter debate followed, after which those who were opposed to the declaration went to the gallery, while those in favor remained on the floor. When heads were counted it was found that the motion had lost by a vote of 57 to 53 with many abstaining. When the meeting reconvened a fortnight later, the controversy continued. After hours of angry discussion sixty ministers went to the gallery, subscribed their support of the Trinity, and left the hall in protest to form their own group. Efforts at reconciliation failed, with the result that two sets of "Advices" later were sent to Exeter: one from the subscribers, with seventy-eight signatures, the other from the nonsubscribers, with seventy-three. The latter set was accompanied by a statement affirming the Trinity, disowning Arianism, and listing their reasons for not subscribing.

The two sets of "Advices" were similar in content, and the differences between the two groups were not theological (there were probably only two Arians in attendance); rather, the controversy was between those who believed that subscription to a doctrinal statement should be required for Christian fellowship (thus they were called "subscribers") and those who did not (the "nonsubscribers"). The disagreement cut across denominational lines as well, though the majority of Independents were subscribers, the majority of Presbyterians nonsubscribers, with the Baptists almost equally divided.

The Salters' Hall conference had the opposite effect from that which was intended, ending with divisions among the Dissenters that were never healed. An extended period of realignment followed, during which subscribers gravitated to nonsubscribers, nonsubscribers to subscribers, the names Presbyterian and Independent gradually lost their original meanings, and the Baptists went off in two different directions. In time, many of the old Presbyterian chapels became Congregational and the old Independent chapels Unitarian. The Salters' Hall conference should be remembered, however, not only for the controversy it provoked, but also because it marked a significant point in the development of free religious thought. Speaking of the nonsubscribers, one church leader stated, "This should always be remembered to their honor, as being the only instance, perhaps, that can be produced out of church history, for many centuries, of any synod of ministers declaring in favor of religious liberty."

From the time of the Salters' Hall Controversy to the end of the eighteenth century the nonsubscribing congregations for the most part went their separate ways, opposed to ecclesiastical domination and firmly committed to individual freedom of belief. "Their ministers," wrote Earl Morse Wilbur, "in general far outstripped those of the other Dissenting churches in ability and scholarship, as their laity also did in culture, wealth, and social influence, . . . [but] they had no acknowledged leader and no accepted plan for the future, and they were not increasing in numbers or strength. In short, they were like a ship that has outridden a heavy storm and reached calm waters, but is now hardly more than drifting, with no captain at the helm and no port in view." It would not be long, however, before the winds of change would bring movement and new direction.

British Unitarianism:
Its Emergence and Maturation as a Movement

"To Truth, to Liberty, to Religion"

—MOTTO, MANCHESTER COLLEGE, 1786

*W*hile Theophilus Lindsey, with the help of his wife Hannah and a few friends, did indeed organize the first Unitarian congregation in England, his example failed to inspire an exodus from the Anglican Church. He may have hoped that, after Parliament had rejected the Feathers Tavern petition from reform-minded Anglicans, many would have followed his lead, but few did, and of those few only four became Unitarians. His intention was "to gather a church of Unitarian Christians out of the Established Church," but in this he failed. It was from the liberal Dissenters, the spiritual descendants of those who had refused to accept the Act of Uniformity in 1662, not from dissident Anglicans, that the Unitarian movement emerged.

However, the congregation that Lindsey had organized in 1774, Essex Street Chapel, continued to prosper—indeed, it has survived to this day—and by 1783 it was able to engage an associate minister; thereafter Lindsey was able to devote much of his time to promoting the Unitarian cause through his writings and personal contacts. Especially important to the future of that cause was his close friendship with Joseph Priestley, who was to become the most influential figure in the early Unitarian movement. Lindsey staunchly defended Priestley's radical views when they came under orthodox attack; these views in turn had a liberalizing effect on Lindsey's own theology, leading him to accept the full humanity of

Christ unencumbered by any supernatural elements. Lindsey was not by nature a controversialist; his opposition to the traditional doctrines regarding God and Christ was based not only on their lack of scriptural foundation, but also on their being barriers to true worship. Thus he did not hesitate to condemn worship of Christ as sheer idolatry, and he narrowed the definition of Unitarianism to the doctrine "that religious worship is to be addressed only to the One True God, the Father." Previously Unitarianism had been regarded as including such unorthodox beliefs as Arianism (that Christ is divine but not equal with God) and Socinianism (that Christ is not divine but can still be invoked in worship). In 1805 Lindsey was forced to resign his ministry at Essex Street because of declining health, dying three years later at the age of eighty-five. He was not a great or original thinker, but through his earnest, persistent efforts he helped to lay the foundation for a new denomination. Whereas in 1790 there had been but two Unitarian congregations in England (his own in London and Priestley's in Birmingham), by 1810 there were twenty, and thereafter the number grew rapidly.

Joseph Priestley stands as one of the outstanding embodiments of the Enlightenment, that cultural movement blending philosophy, science, and reason which in England, as in America, provided the substrate for the emergence of liberal religious thought. He was forty-seven when in 1780 he was chosen to fill the pulpit of the New Meeting in Birmingham, perhaps the most liberal church in all England. By that time he had held a rich variety of positions—that of Dissenting minister to both rural and urban congregations, as well as schoolmaster, academy tutor, writer, and librarian and literary companion to an earl. His interests were likewise varied and rich—chemistry (he discovered oxygen without realizing that he had), politics, theology, philosophy, and literature.

Through his frequent stays in London he became acquainted with the leading Dissenters, deepened his friendship with the Lindseys, and met some of the most prominent scientists and statesmen of the day, including Benjamin Franklin who became his close friend. In all his endeavors he was supported by his wife Mary—"one of the best wives a minister ever had," the historian Alexander Gordon called her. "Married at the age of eighteen, she proved herself an unequalled housewife; . . . took from her husband every domestic care; . . . drew him punctually from his laboratory for that evening game of skill, which was her bright hour and his, at the close of every busy day; stuck to her old-fashioned Arianism through all his heresies, not from mere use and wont, for she was a woman of culture and reading; and with a most dainty and incisive pen, wrote the best letter of any woman of her time."

The congregation of the New Meeting gave Priestley a great deal of freedom, expecting only that he preach and give religious instruction to the young people on Sunday. Because a colleague associate was responsible for pastoral and weekday duties, Priestley could devote the rest of the time to his chemical experiments, study, and writing. He soon made the acquaintance of the leading scholars and scientists of the city. On their invitation he became a member of the Lunar Society, so-called because it met in the homes of its members on the Monday closest to the full moon so that after the meeting adjourned they could find their way home.

Of Priestley's many published writings two made an especially great impact both in England and on the Continent. In his *Corruptions of Christianity* and *History of Early Opinions concerning Jesus Christ,* he made a strong case that the early Christian church had held a unitarian view of God and a humanistic view of Christ, a thesis that drew strong and persistent condemnation from the orthodox. At first Lindsey and the liberal Dissenters, mostly Arian in theology, were alarmed by Priestley's radical position, particularly his thoroughgoing determinism, which rejected free will, and his materialism, which rejected any concept of spirit or soul; everything depended for its existence, he claimed, on physical substances. His beliefs were a strange mixture of the orthodox and the heretical—he accepted the miracles of Jesus, but not the virgin birth; accepted the physical resurrection of the body, but not the existence of the soul. Nevertheless, persuaded by his arguments and emboldened by his courage, many of the Dissenters in time came to accept openly much, even if not all, of his views. Thus in converting many of his coreligionists to Unitarianism, Joseph Priestley succeeded where Theophilus Lindsey had failed.

Meanwhile the French Revolution had broken out in 1789, and Priestley, like many Dissenters, gave it his open support just as he had the American Revolution thirteen years earlier. Ever since the revolution of 1688 that forced James II from the throne, the Dissenters had celebrated its anniversary by holding a dinner on November 5 at which a toast was drunk to "civil and religious liberty the world over." Thus it was not surprising that this new revolution would inspire a similar celebration, and accordingly in 1791 a dinner was planned for Birmingham on Bastille Day (July 14).

By then, however, hostility to the Dissenters in general and Priestley in particular had mounted on both political and theological grounds. Opposition to the French Revolution, led by Edmund Burke, and to unorthodox theology, led by the Anglican High Church party, had created a confrontational climate in which an eruption became almost inevitable. On Bastille Day an angry crowd gathered outside the hotel in Birmingham where the celebration had been scheduled to take place. By then, however, the dinner was over and the guests, some eighty in number, had already departed. Someone in the frustrated crowd shouted, "To the New Meeting!" The mob then rushed to the chapel and set it on fire, after which the other Unitarian church in the city, the Old Meeting, was looted. Next rose the cry, "To Dr. Priestley's!" Priestley, who had not attended the dinner, managed to escape with his family before the mob arrived, but his home and laboratory were looted and set on fire. The loss was devastating to the couple. Mary "had stitched with her own hands every bed-curtain and window-curtain in their . . . house, and she had seen her needlework in a blaze." Late that night, warned that Joseph's life was still in danger, the couple were driven out of town to safety; they never saw Birmingham again.

The riots continued for three days, until they were finally broken up by troops sent from London. The local authorities then posted notices saluting the rioters as "Friends and Fellow Churchmen" and requesting that, for their own best interest, they should destroy no more homes; few were ever punished. Later it became evident that the riot had been instigated as part of a careful plan devised by the High Church party, marking the chapels and homes of the leading Dissenters for destruction. Fortunately the rest of the plan was not carried out; it was considered that the Dissenters had already been taught a lesson. While the Dissenters had indeed suffered a setback, it proved to be only temporary; over the long run the Birmingham Riots and the conservative support they received played a formative role in the Unitarian movement, sharpening distinctions and bringing a spirit of unity to its supporters.

The Priestleys found a safe haven first in London, then in Clapton, and finally in Hackney, where Joseph became minister of the Gravel Pit Meeting. He had wanted to return to Birmingham on the Sunday following the riots and preach on the importance of forgiveness, but he was dissuaded by his friends, who convinced him that this would be too dangerous; instead, his sermon was read by the minister of the Old Meeting. While shunned by many (no word of sympathy or support came from the Church of England), his friends rallied round him, giving their moral and financial support. His *Appeal to the Public*, published in two parts, gave a full account of the causes and conduct of the riots and a strong vindication of himself and others against the charge of disloyalty and sedition.

Nevertheless, in February 1794, Priestley presented his resignation to the Gravel Pit congregation, announcing his decision to leave England and go to America. For one thing, the French Revolution had degenerated into the Reign of Terror, and Priestley, commonly thought to be still supporting the Revolution, was viewed with increasing suspicion; he and Tom Paine, who had written in support of the Revolution, were frequently being burned in effigy, and there was no guarantee of his safety. In addition, his three sons, unable to find positions in England, had already migrated to America, and his wife Mary was anxious to follow them. "I do not think," she had written a friend, "that God can require it of us as a duty, after they have smote one cheek, to turn the other. I am for trying a new soil." "Joseph," she was to say later, "we pack for America."

In early April the couple set sail, arriving in New York after eight weeks at sea. From there they traveled on to Philadelphia, which was then not only the political capital of the new nation, but its intellectual capital as well. Benjamin Franklin had died four years earlier, but there Priestley made the acquaintance of George Washington, John Adams, Thomas Jefferson, Benjamin Rush, and other of the country's leaders. He quickly became acquainted with the Universalists in the city, helped them to raise money for a new meetinghouse, and frequently occupied their pulpit. Since he agreed with them "concerning the final salvation of all the human race," he might be considered as one of the first Unitarian Universalists! While in Philadelphia Priestley was largely responsible for the establishment of the First Unitarian Church there. Then after he had moved westward to join his sons in Northumberland, a frontier town on the Susquehanna River, he established a Unitarian chapel and served as its minister. Mary, who had never completely recovered from the trauma of the riots, died in 1796; Joseph lived until 1804, staying active with his ministry and chemical experiments and keeping up his correspondence with Lindsey almost to the end.

Joseph Priestley arrived in the New World only a decade before the Unitarian Controversy broke out in New England, in which liberal and orthodox Congregationalists split, the liberals becoming Unitarians. Nevertheless, his influence on the emergence of Unitarianism in America was small. Unlike John Murray, who had crossed the Atlantic a quarter of a century earlier with his message of Universalism, Priestley inspired no sweeping movement; his theology was too scientific, too materialistic to have broad appeal. In fact, most of the Unitarians in New England, where American Unitarianism has its roots, took pains to distance themselves from his views. For instance, the "father" of American Unitarianism, William Ellery Channing, while admiring him, rejected his theology. "With Dr. Priestley, a good and great man, . . . ," he wrote, "I have less sympathy than with the 'Orthodox.'" Thus any attempts to link American Unitarianism with that of European, other than through their common origins in the Enlightenment, are strained at best.

Interestingly, only a few years before the Unitarian Joseph Priestley crossed the Atlantic from England to America, the Universalist Elhanan Winchester of Philadelphia crossed in the opposite direction. He helped William Vidler initiate a lively but short-lived Universalist movement in England, but by 1825 it had been absorbed almost completely into the growing Unitarian denomination.

At the turn of the century English Unitarians found themselves in a precarious position. Both the established church and the political conservatives regarded them with suspicion and hostility; they were scattered, with no effective means of communication to unite them; and, with Priestley gone to America and Lindsey growing old, they found themselves without a leader. Fortunately one emerged in the person of Thomas Belsham, the most prominent of the orthodox Dissenters to become a Unitarian. After reluctantly thinking his way through to a Unitarian position he had resigned as divinity tutor at an orthodox academy, planning to retire to private life. However, Priestley and Lindsey, who had both come to know him over the years, pressed him into accepting a position as resident tutor at the New College at Hackney, a Dissenters' institution.

During his five years there Belsham helped organize the Unitarian Society for Promoting Christian Knowledge and the Practice of Virtue by the Distribution of Books (commonly referred to as the Unitarian Book Society), to be supported by those who affirmed the proper unity of God and simple humanity of Christ. Thus Arians were excluded from participation, since for them Christ was more than simply human, and indeed Arianism, which had never found an institutional home, died out rapidly thereafter, with many Arian ministers coming over to the Unitarian ranks. When Priestley resigned his Gravel Pit pulpit in Hackney, the congregation unanimously chose Belsham, who in general shared his friend's theological views, to succeed him. Then a decade later he was elected minister of Lindsey's Essex Street Chapel in London, a position he held until his death in 1829.

With the zeal of a new convert and skills as an organizer, writer, and preacher, Thomas Belsham gave the growing Unitarian movement strong leadership through the first quarter of the nineteenth century. He was a courageous and effective controversialist, answering the many orthodox attacks forthrightly both from the pulpit and in writing. His *A Calm Inquiry into the Scripture Doctrine concerning the Person of Christ*, carefully setting forth the scriptural argument for the Unitarian position, appeared in 1811, his *Memoirs of Theophilus Lindsey*, a year later. When in 1813 the so-called Trinity Act was passed, finally ending penalties against deniers of the Trinity, Belsham replied to those who denounced its enactment with a skillful mixture of politeness and withering sarcasm. Later, when an Anglican bishop attacked "persons calling themselves Unitarians," including those in the Welsh congregations, he published *A Letter to the Unitarian Christians in South Wales* in their support. The last of his many replies to the orthodox was directed at the Bampton Lectures, a prestigious endowed series at Oxford; but in 1818 the lectures were so full of dogmatism, ignorance, and abuse leveled against the Unitarians that Belsham felt called upon to refute them in detail. Thereafter, with his health beginning to decline, he served the movement through his Essex Street congregation in less demanding ways.

The Unitarian movement was strengthened during this period by the addition of both congregations and individual leaders from the General Baptists, so-called because they believed that Christ died for all believers, not just for the elect. They were the spiritual descendants of the Anabaptists, many of whom were antitrinitarians in their beliefs. In 1770 the General Baptists had divided into orthodox and liberal camps. Some fifty congregations gradually merged with the Unitarians while at the same time retaining their Baptist name, holding their own separate assemblies, and continuing their tradition of baptism by immersion.

Among those liberal General Baptists were Robert Aspland, David Eaton, and Richard Wright, each of whom was to make a unique contribution to the Unitarian movement. Aspland, who had begun his ministry with the General Baptists on the Isle of Wight and had gone on to succeed Belsham at Hackney, was responsible, with the help of William Vidler, for establishing the *Monthly Repository* as the first regularly appearing Unitarian journal, thereby establishing an effective communications network within the new denomination. Eaton, born in Scotland of humble parents, was a shoemaker with little education. He became associated with a Baptist congregation at York and soon became an effective lay preacher. Later, after moving to London as a bookseller, he urged influential Unitarians to initiate a program of missionary preaching to the humbler classes. Predictably there were objections: the time was not ripe, Unitarianism was not a religion for the masses, the Unitarian Book Society was already meeting this need, to cite a few. But after eight years of persistent urging by Eaton, the Unitarian Fund for Promoting Unitarianism by means of Popular Preaching was organized in 1806. Under the direction of an able committee with Aspland as its energetic secretary, the Fund received broad support and soon engaged Richard

Wright, a General Baptist minister at Wisbeach, as its part-time missionary.

Wright, like Vidler, had moved from Calvinism to Unitarianism by way of Universalism. By 1810 the program had proved so successful that Wright resigned his pastorate in order to devote himself full time to his missionary work among working people, a ministry he continued for the next twelve years. During that period he traveled some 3,000 miles a year on foot in every part of England, Scotland, and Wales, preaching in 400 or 500 different places, in many of them more than once. In the process he helped organize or reopen scores of churches, especially in manufacturing districts, and brought a new spirit and breadth to the whole denomination.

On May 26, 1825, the British and Foreign Unitarian Association was organized, incorporating the Unitarian Fund within it. (By coincidence the American Unitarian Association was established on that same day.) By then there were more than 200 congregations in England, 34 in Wales, and 12 in Scotland; only fifteen years earlier there had been but a score. In addition, the Non-Subscribing Presbyterians in Ireland, mostly Arian in theology, were on the verge of forming their own organization. Belsham (who would die just four years later), Aspland, Eaton, Wright, and many others could look back with satisfaction to what had been accomplished.

While the British and Foreign Unitarian Association was envisaged as an organization of both individuals and congregations, only a small minority of the latter ever chose to join, evidently fearing a loss of independence. As a result, in 1867 the Association abolished the category of congregational membership, and thereafter was composed wholly of individuals. It took seriously its identification as a foreign as well as a British institution, making a concerted attempt to reach out to liberal religious groups in other countries, including Germany, France, Gibraltar, and, as previously mentioned, Transylvania and Hungary. Some of its most important foreign work was in India, where it helped to establish a Unitarian mission and to support the indigenous movement led by Rammohun Roy that resulted in the formation of the Brahmo Samaj. In the middle years of the nineteenth century, permanent churches were established in such important colonial centers as Montreal and Toronto in Canada; Sydney, Melbourne, and Adelaide in Australia; Hobart in Tasmania; and Cape Town in South Africa.

Meanwhile, the success of the Unitarians on the home front prompted their orthodox opponents to challenge their right not only to many of their chapels, but also to some sources of financial support. Back in 1704, Dame Sarah Hewley, a Presbyterian of York, had founded a charity for the benefit "of poor and godly preachers of Christ's holy Gospel"; over the years the fund had grown to a value of more than £100,000. Lady Hewley had imposed no doctrinal requirements, and in the course of time the administration of the fund had passed into Unitarian hands, with its income benefiting Unitarian causes. In 1830 a group of Independents brought suit against the trustees, claiming that control of the fund should be given to orthodox Dissenters. Proceedings dragged on for twelve years, but the court finally ruled in favor of the complainants on the grounds that a trust could not be held for any use that would have been illegal at the time it was established. "The decision of the case," wrote Earl Morse Wilbur, "gave unfeigned delight to the orthodox, but filled the Unitarians with dismay."

The orthodox quickly took steps to challenge control of another large Presbyterian fund, the Dr. Williams's Trust, and the Unitarians feared that title to as many as 200 of their chapels might soon be challenged. Fortunately the Attorney-General, unhappy with the Lady Hewley ruling, refused to sanction this Trust suit, and the Dissenters' Chapel Act, passed by Parliament in 1844, guaranteed that title to the chapels would be retained by their occupants on the principle that long, uncontested possession creates a vested right.

With their chapels and funds secure at last from orthodox takeover, the Unitarians entered a new phase of optimism and growth, with many of the old chapels repaired and new ones built. Moreover, two new sources of funds had largely offset the loss of financial resources resulting from the Lady Hewley case: a new trust endowed by Robert Hibbert, a wealthy London merchant, and the establishment of a Ministers' Stipend Augmentation Fund. Out of this new, hopeful environment a missionary spirit emerged, particularly in the growing manufacturing towns of the northern county of Lancashire, where there was a need for ministers who could relate well to the working class. As a result, a new school for training ministers was established at Manchester in 1854 under the name of the Unitarian Home Missionary Board. Its aim was to prepare for the ministry those who had no college degrees but had backgrounds in the trades or industry. Begun as an experiment, the school enjoyed immediate success and has survived as one of the two centers in Britain preparing men and women for the Unitarian ministry. In 1889 it was renamed the Unitarian Home Missionary College, and, in 1926, Unitarian College, Manchester.

Up until the founding of the new school, Unitarian ministers had for the most part been educated at Manchester College, established in Manchester in 1786. Since then, the college has led a peripatetic existence, moving to York in 1803, back to Manchester in 1840, to London in 1853 (just before the new school opened), and to Oxford in 1889. Presently it is known as Harris Manchester College, Oxford. From the start, the college has placed a strong emphasis on scholarship, with most of those admitted already holding baccalaureate degrees.

James Martineau, considered by many as the most important figure in nineteenth-century British Unitarianism, was intimately connected with Manchester College for most of his long life. Educated for the ministry at the college when it was located in York, he served churches in Dublin and Liverpool, but his most important contribution to the movement was as a faculty member at the college from 1840 until 1885, the last sixteen as its principal. During his tenure his thinking underwent significant change, influenced by the advent of Darwinism, Idealist philosophy, and biblical higher criticism, in which questions of interpretation and historical accuracy are applied to the Bible. During Martineau's student days, Unitarians were convinced that their theology, based on the thought of such men as Lindsey, Priestley, and Belsham, was more in accord with the Bible than was that of the orthodox. Charles Wellbeloved, the college's principal, had expressed a view commonly held by Unitarians when he wrote in a controversy with an orthodox opponent, "Convince us that any tenet is authorized by the Bible, from that moment we receive it, . . . and no power on earth shall wrest it from us."

With the passage of time, however, Martineau, significantly influenced by the writings of the Americans William Ellery Channing and Theodore Parker, was among those who became convinced that the Bible was inadequate as a theological base. In 1848 he had gone abroad for a year, spent chiefly in Germany studying philosophy and New Testament criticism; the experience helped move him further away from a biblical theology toward the intuitional, spiritual theology he was to adopt. He urged Unitarians to move not only beyond biblicism, but also beyond rationalism, scientism, and materialism toward a "religion of the Spirit" in which men and women can directly experience "life with God"; in this he came close to the views of the American Transcendentalists.

Many saw Martineau as having abandoned the essentials of the Unitarian faith; they were critical, too, of his open condemnation of Unitarianism as being too narrow. In fact, Martineau, though a Unitarian in theology, would never consent to join as member or minister any church that bore the Unitarian name. He saw the name as implying a particular theological position rather than the openness that he felt to be essential. In the 1860s he led an effort to form a broad inclusive union of all liberal churches on a spiritual basis regardless of doctrinal differences, but the Unitarian press was hostile and the attempt failed. Martineau's effort was entirely consistent with the college's philosophy, for it had never been an exclusively Unitarian institution; instead it was broadly liberal in character and open to students of all denominations. At the time of his retirement he expressed his disappointment with both the denomination and cultural trends in a letter to a friend:

> Whatever aspects of truth we may have saved from neglect, whatever spiritual resources we may have rendered more accessible . . . need another administration before they lay hold of the minds and hearts of men. It is the power of Faith that shall prevail. We have it not, except as a feeble residuum from the power of criticism. . . .
>
> Unitarianism continued to draw ministers and laymen from other denominations, but there was a larger movement or drift away. Far more threatening was a growing skepticism or indifference, reinforced in the general culture by more satisfying intellectual explanations and by the competition offered by the multiplication of ways of spending time and engaging enthusiasm, even on Sunday.

Evidently, in Martineau's mind the secularization of British culture was already well under way. Nevertheless, despite his disappointment, he continued to be a strong supporter of the college, serving as president of its trustees for two years following his retirement from its faculty and participating in the dedication of the college's chapel in Oxford in 1893. He was a prolific writer, and several of his books were published in the years surrounding or following his retirement. In 1888 he made one last attempt to organize an inclusive organization of liberal churches in Britain and Ireland under the nondoctrinal name of Presbyterian; others listened to him with respect, but again rejected his plan. James Martineau's impact on the Unitarian movement was profound, nevertheless. His followers, most of whom were unwilling to abandon the Unitarian name, represented a liberalizing wing in the denomination that saw the need for openness and change—a need that persisted into the next century. Just as that new century was beginning, Martineau died, widely respected and full of years, in 1900 at the age of ninety-four.

As the old century was drawing to a close, it was evident that Martineau's pessimism with regard to Unitarianism was not widely shared. There were some 360 congregations in Britain, and their membership included many national and civic leaders; attendance was high; new sanctuaries were being built; a National Conference of Unitarian, Liberal Christian, Free Christian, Presbyterian, and other Non-Subscribing or Kindred Congregations had been organized in 1882 as a deliberative body meeting triennially; a new headquarters for the British and Foreign Unitarian Association had been built in 1885 at the site of Lindsey's old Essex Street Chapel (the congregation had moved to Kensington); and relocation of Manchester College to Oxford was seen as a harbinger of greater things to come. British Unitarians entered the twentieth century with optimism and hope.

The Twentieth Century: A Brief Overview

The International Association for Religious Freedom affirms the one Spirit of life in which we have our being and the openness to diverse expressions of faith and wisdom which is necessary for spiritual growth. We seek the realization of our true nature and justice and peace in the world.

—IARF AFFIRMATION, 1994

*I*t was appropriate that the International Association for Religious Freedom (IARF) should have been organized in 1900, for the new century just beginning was to be marked by increasing communication and cooperation between Unitarians and other religious liberals throughout the world. The Unitarian Church of Hungary, the British and Foreign Unitarian Association, the American Unitarian Association, and the Universalist General Convention (later renamed the Universalist Church of America) were all among its original members. Over the years the IARF has provided a framework in which European Unitarians have come into regular contact with each other; with their American, Canadian, Australian, New Zealand, and Asian counterparts; and with those from non-Western faith traditions. The twentieth century, of course, also has brought with it two world wars that have had a global impact, and nowhere was this impact more devastating than in Europe; the Unitarians in Hungary, Romania, and Great Britain were inevitably and profoundly affected by both these conflicts, as were those in Czechoslovakia.

The century began well for the Hungarian Unitarians, however. They started new denominational periodicals, published books, and held a magnificent celebration in 1910 marking the four-hundredth anniversary of Francis Dávid's birth, even though the actual year of his birth remains uncertain. In connection with this celebration, a plaque was dedicated at the castle in Déva bearing the following inscription:

> In the dungeon of the Déva fortress Dávid Ferenc, the founder and the bishop of the Unitarian Church, was condemned to life imprisonment because of his religious conviction, and passed away in 1579. Placed in 1910 with reverence on the 400th anniversary of his birth by his spiritual successor, the Unitarian Church.

Four years later the First World War erupted, with Hungary taking sides with Germany; Romania tried to remain aloof, but eventually joined the Allies. Church life in both countries was disrupted as men were pressed into military service, and church bells and organ pipes were confiscated to make armaments. When the armistice was declared in 1918, Romanian troops occupied Transylvania and proceeded to pillage the countryside. Then in 1921, Transylvania was ceded to Romania under the Treaty of Trianon as a prize of war. Ever since then the Transylvanian Hungarians have been an often-persecuted minority, living under a government controlled by people with an ethnic and religious background quite different from their own. With national borders redrawn, the Unitarian churches in Hungary, relatively few in number, found themselves isolated from those in Transylvania; a deputy-bishop, responsible to the Transylvanian bishop in Kolozsvár, was appointed to serve them.

Following the treaty, the treatment of the Transylvanians by the Romanians brought strong protests from the Unitarian, Reformed, Lutheran, and Catholic bishops. (The Romanians are predominantly Eastern Orthodox.) Among those responding to these protests were Unitarians from Great Britain and America, who sent a number of commissions to investigate conditions and report their findings. One of the greatest problems that was identified stemmed from the agrarian reform program in Romania, whereby the government confiscated large estates and redistributed the land in arbitrary ways. To help their fellow Unitarians in this period of crisis, many American and British congregations adopted Transylvanian congregations through a "sister church" program and provided them with financial and moral support. Bishop József Ferencz led the Transylvanian Unitarians during much of this difficult period; later, from the time of his death in 1928 until the end of the Second World War, three different men held this office: György Boros, Béla Varga, and Miklos Józan.

The situation for the Transylvanian Unitarians gradually was improving when, in 1939, war broke out again, with both Hungary and Romania being occupied by the Germans. To lessen the friction between the two neighboring countries, the boundaries between them were revised, with part of Transylvania restored (temporarily, as it developed) to Hungary. Thus after more than two decades many Unitarian churches found themselves freed from Romanian control, although more than fifty remained in Romania. It was not long, however, before the Unitarian churches' close ties to their British and American coreligionists brought them under suspicion with the German authorities. Some ministers were imprisoned or sent to concentration camps, church incomes from landed property were drastically reduced, the three churches in Budapest were nearly destroyed, and one Transylvanian village was completely wiped out.

The Unitarians demonstrated much heroism during the German occupation; Alexander Szent-Iványi, former minister in Kolozsvár, deserves particular mention for his work in Budapest helping the many refugees, securing humane treatment for prisoners of war, and establishing hospital care for those with medical needs. When finally peace was restored in 1945 he became deputy-bishop of the Unitarian churches in Hungary. At the end of the war Carleton Fisher, an American

Universalist minister working in Hungary on behalf of the Unitarian and Universalist Service Committees, helped to establish child-feeding and crop-growing programs until he was forced out by the new Communist government; in Romania, too, the government soon came under Communist control. National boundaries were again redrawn, with all of Transylvania and parts of eastern Hungary coming under Romanian rule.

For more than forty years the Communist governments in both Hungary and Romania closely watched and regulated the Unitarian churches; the oppression in Romania was particularly heavy. Government workers and their families were discouraged from attending church services; Communist-controlled "cultural centers" were built even in small villages, designed to replace the churches as the center of community life; religious instruction was banned from the schools; and the government assumed the right to confiscate any church property. The number of Unitarian ecclesiastical districts was reduced from eight to five, and the Unitarian theological seminary in Kolozsvár, founded in 1915, was forced to merge with the Reformed and Lutheran schools to form a single Protestant Theological Institute, with the size of its student body greatly restricted. For a dozen years those living in Hungary were not permitted to attend the new seminary.

Later, in the early 1960s, after President Nicolae Ceausescu had come to power in Romania, ministers and seminarians who refused to make the necessary ideological compromises required by the Communist state were brought to trial. Some twenty of them were imprisoned, and on their release ministers were often assigned to churches where their influence would be minimal. One such minister, Imre Gellérd, who persisted in following the dictates of his conscience, finally ended his own life early in 1980 rather than face another arrest and imprisonment; seventy of his ministerial colleagues jeopardized their own standing by attending his funeral. Indeed, the question of how far a minister should go in cooperating with the Communist authorities was a continuing and wrenching one; on the one hand lay the matter of personal integrity and conscience, on the other hand the matter of continuing one's ministry and serving one's church.

Nevertheless, the Communist government kept up a pretense of being supportive of religion. The constitution of the Romanian Socialist Republic, adopted in 1965, guaranteed to every citizen freedom of conscience and the free practice of religion, a guarantee with little substance since its interpretation was left to the Communist authorities. Then three years later President Ceausescu called together the leaders of all the denominations in the country, among them Elek Kiss, who had served as Unitarian bishop since 1946. Ceausescu expressed his deep appreciation to the leaders for the work of their churches, then required them all to take an oath to support the "noble work of the state." (One recalls the words of Superintendent Demetrius Hunyadi, spoken almost four centuries earlier: "My friends, be adaptable. The condition of our continued survival is constant adaptation.")

Though carefully watched and significantly restricted, the life of the Unitarian Church continued. Later that same year a Unitarian General Assembly was held at Kolozsvár, Torda, and Déva to celebrate the four-hundredth anniversary of the Act of Religious Toleration and the founding of Unitarianism under Francis Dávid; representatives of the Unitarian Universalist Association, the British General Assembly of Unitarian and Free Christian Churches, and the IARF were among those in attendance. Bishop Kiss had previously visited the majority of the churches, emphasizing the importance of the occasion, and many had made major renovations and repairs to their buildings as a result. In appreciation for his leadership, Kiss received honorary doctorates that year from both the Protestant Theological Seminary in Kolozsvár and the Meadville/ Lombard Theological School in Chicago. After his death in 1971 he was succeeded as bishop by Lajos Kovács, who in 1975 was elected president of the IARF.

Conditions for the vast majority of those living in Romania became increasingly difficult during the years of the Ceausescu regime. For the Hungarians in Transylvania, life became especially difficult as they were singled out for discrimination as aliens in a Romanian culture. Cities and towns that had been primarily Hungarian became dominated by Romanians relocated by the government to effect cultural change; the city of Kolozsvár, long a Hungarian and Unitarian center, was one such casualty. At the same time, the whole structure of village life was undermined as farmland was collectivized and dormitories were built to house agricultural workers.

Meanwhile the national birth rate rose rapidly as a consequence of programs to increase the population (for example, abortion had been made illegal); as a result, thousands of unwanted children were warehoused in government-run orphanages. Pollution, too, increased rapidly as factories sought to meet government-imposed production goals. Informers reported those who failed to cooperate with government policies, and, as implied earlier, the Unitarian ministry became seriously divided over the issue of collaboration versus resistance. American Unitarian Universalists and British Unitarians were among those who viewed the deteriorating conditions with concern but felt helpless to turn the tide. Then suddenly in December 1989 the people revolted. The Communist government was overturned, Ceausescu and his wife were summarily executed, and the country reorganized as a Socialist democracy.

Though the change was welcomed, the attempt to move from a dictatorship to a democracy and from Communism to a free market economy has proved extraordinarily difficult. Discrimination against the Hungarian minority, including the Unitarians, continued; many of the new national leaders were former Communists who continued to think in their old ways and to regard Hungarians with suspicion. For example, the police forces in villages, towns, and cities that ethnically are Hungarian have been made up largely of Romanians. Then in

1995 the Romanian National Assembly enacted a law that established Romanian as the dominant language of instruction in most schools, including those that were Hungarian-speaking by tradition. In addition, the government suspended its program under which property confiscated by the Communist regime was being returned to the churches; at the same time it increased support for the Romanian Orthodox Church, now officially established as the national church. János Erdö, a former political prisoner who succeeded Lajos Kovács as Bishop of the Unitarian Church of Romania in 1994, considered the relationship between the Romanians and the Hungarian minority to be one of the two greatest problems facing his church.

Bishop Erdö, who died suddenly in July 1996, considered the other major problem to be that of reinstituting religious training in the schools, which had been an important means of educating young people about their faith prior to the secularization of education under the Communists. While there have been some instances in which this reinstitution has been carried out partially (as at the Orbán Balázs Gymnasium at Székelykeresztúr, founded by the Unitarians in 1793), and while Unitarian ministers are again teaching religion to Unitarian students in some schools, there remains much to be done.

Nevertheless, during this post-Communist period, Unitarianism has been slowly regaining hope for the future. As of April 1996, there were approximately 80,000 Unitarians in Romania, well over half of them in village churches (this number includes all those in Unitarian families regardless of age and degree of church involvement); there were some 130 churches, all except two within Transylvania itself; five new churches were being built, in Barót, Sepsiszentgyörgy, Székelyudvarhely (where 6,000 Unitarians were too many for one church and one minister!), Marosszentgyörgy, and Fehérgyháza; there were thirty-one Unitarian students enrolled in the Protestant Theological Seminary in Kolozsvár; and two denominational publications of high quality were appearing regularly: the quarterly journal *Keresztény Magvetö*

("Christian Seed-Sower") and the monthy newsletter *Unitárius Közlöny* ("Unitarian Gazette").

In a male-dominated culture—in which church councils traditionally have been composed entirely of men, the sexes have sat separately during church services, and the men have been served first during communion—changes have slowly begun to take place. Nine of the seminarians during the 1995-96 academic year were women, three women ministers previously had been settled in congregations, and in the city churches men and women have begun sitting together. (Among the women serving as ministers has been Aniko Harrington, wife of retired American minister Donald Harrington. Her aunt, the late Vilma Szantho Harrington, like Aniko a native of Transylvania and Donald's first wife, for many years did much to promote American interest in the Transylvanian Unitarians.)

Change, however, has come slowly, not only because of cultural resistance and governmental repression, but also because of the deep commitment of Transylvanian Unitarians to the preservation of their tradition—a tradition that has held them together for more than four centuries. Their worship services are Reformed Christian in character, regularly including the Lord's Prayer. The Lord's Table, from which communion is served four times each year, is the focal center of their churches. Sermons are based on biblical texts, and hymns are for the most part solemn in tone, reflecting the long years of oppression through which they have suffered. In many ways Transylvanian Unitarianism resembles nineteenth-century American Unitarianism; in fact, William Ellery Channing, Ralph Waldo Emerson, and Theodore Parker continue to be sources of inspiration and theological insight.

To some American visitors, the Transylvanian Unitarians have appeared conservative (even "un-Unitarian" to the least sensitive), but given their history and the culture within which they exist, they are in fact genuinely liberal and humanistic, by far the most progressive, hopeful, forward-looking religious body in Romania. They are not pietistic; their faith is instead for them a way of life. For the most part their churches are full only on the communion Sundays at Harvest Thanksgiving, Christmas, Easter, and Pentecost, and on Confirmation Sundays when youth are welcomed into full church membership. Their Christ is a human Christ whose suffering they understand, and their God is the single creative, sustaining source of all life and being. *"Egy az Isten"* ("God is One") remains their motto, and Francis Dávid remains their martyr-hero; the picture of him arguing for religious tolerance at the Diet of Torda adorns the walls of their churches. Imre Gellérd described well the substance and sources of their faith in these words:

> It must be considered positive that our preachers have escaped from the spirit of resignation, desperation, losing heart, passivity, alienation, exaltation, ill-fantasy, sectarianism, and antihumanism as a consequence of suffering. . . . *[O]ur religion was able to produce one of the most optimistic, constructive, and humanistic religious systems.* . . . Through suffering, special powers and qualities are born in us: unity, solidarity, strong faith, adequate self-knowledge, a sense of historical orientation.

Ties between North American Unitarian Universalist congregations and Unitarian congregations in Romania have been greatly strengthened in recent years through the "Partner Church Project," initiated in 1988 through the leadership of Judit Gellérd, daughter of Imre Gellérd; her husband, George Williams; and William Schulz and Natalie Gulbrandsen, president and moderator of the Unitarian Universalist Association (UUA) at that time. In 1993 a Partner Church Council was organized to coordinate the program. As of 1996 almost every Transylvanian Unitarian church had been linked to a partner church in America, with the latter providing financial, political, and moral support and receiving in return not only gratitude, but also an expanded religious and cultural perspective and a greater appreciation of the importance of tradition and commitment. A number of Transylvanian ministers and their families have paid visits to their partner churches, and many American Unitarian Universalists have visited Transylvania. In the process, bridges of mutual respect, understanding, and friendship have been built. Americans also have provided support to the Unitarian community at the Protestant seminary in Kolozsvár, as well as to Unitarians in Hungary and Czechoslovakia.

The Unitarian Church in Hungary has fared better than that in Romania; the Communist government there, though antireligious, proved considerably less oppressive. Their numbers are small—some 2,000 members divided among eleven churches, the largest in Budapest. Alexander Szent-Iványi served for only one year as their deputy-bishop before leaving in 1947, going first to England, then to America. Soon afterward the Hungarian Church broke off from the Romanian, with József Ferencz, namesake and grandson of the bishop who served for fifty-two years, becoming the first bishop of Hungary in 1971. Recently Ilona Szent-Iványi Orbók became deputy-bishop, the first woman to hold that office.

For the Unitarians in Great Britain, as for those in Hungary, the new century started well, then brought trying times. In addition to two devastating wars, the Unitarians in both lands faced major foes; whereas in Hungary and Romania the foes were Communism and ethnic oppression, in Great Britain they have been the continuing secularization of society and the general decline of institutional religion. While the number of Unitarian congregations and ministers has decreased but slowly, church membership and attendance have dropped alarmingly during the century in spite of some able leadership and periodic efforts to turn the tide. At the beginning of the century there were some 360 congregations and a comparable number of ministers; as of 1995 there were approximately 190 congregations and 140 ministers. No membership figures were kept until around 1945 (presumably there were about 30,000 members in the mid-1920s), but over the last half century the total membership has decreased from approximately 25,000 to 7,000, with attendance figures showing an even sharper decline. These figures do not include the Non-Subscribing Presbyterian congregations in Ireland, which though affiliated with the British Unitarians, have always had a unique status.

The First World War had a devastating effect on British Unitarianism. Its optimistic, progress-oriented theology was found wanting, morale suffered badly, and attendance at Sunday services began a sharp decline. Ever since that time British Unitarians have struggled to find a fresh vision and a theology to go with it. But despite the decline, the work of the churches has gone on. In 1928, in an attempt to bring greater efficiency and vitality to the movement, a thoroughgoing reorganization was effected. At that time the British and Foreign Unitarian Association, founded in 1825, and the National Conference of Unitarian, Liberal Christian, Free Christian, Presbyterian, and Other Non-Subscribing or Kindred Congregations (NCULCFCPONSKC!), founded in 1882, merged to form a delegate body called the General Assembly of Unitarian and Free Christian Churches, with a general secretary as chief administrator. (This consolidation took place in the same year that, on the other side of the Atlantic, the General Conference of Unitarian Churches was being merged with the American Unitarian Association; similarly, the British and Foreign Unitarian Association and the American Unitarian Association both had been organized in 1825.) At the time the General Assembly was formed, a group of four leading ministers was charged with the task of preparing a manifesto declaring what Unitarianism had to offer to the new age; unfortunately and symptomatically, they could come to no agreement. Nor was support for the new organization unanimous; L. P. Jacks and Alexander Gordon, who had often been cited as Unitarian leaders, both declined to have their names included in the official list of ministers.

Mortimer Rowe was chosen as the Assembly's first general secretary and served with distinction from 1929 until 1949. He was followed by John Kielty (1949-69), Brian Golland (1969-79), Roy Smith (1979-94), and Jeffrey Teagle, who took office in 1994. Rowe also made significant contributions by editing an anthology of biblical passages, a hymnal, and a book of worship services. Among the presidents of the Assembly has been J. Chuter Ede, British Home Secretary from 1945 until 1951 and one of the few nationally known Unitarians of the century.

The Second World War also had a devastating effect on British Unitarianism. Of 334 Unitarian church buildings, forty-six were damaged or destroyed by enemy action; repairs were costly, and some churches never were rebuilt. Essex Hall, the denominational headquarters in London on the former site of Theophilus Lindsey's Essex Street Chapel, was among the structures destroyed; it was rebuilt at the same location. (The Essex Street congregation had moved to Kensington in the late nineteenth century.) At war's end the British Unitarians resolved to carry on, as evidenced from a report on "The Work of the Churches," published in 1946:

> Altogether, then, we have considerable resources; 24,000 people with a mission and a purpose, backed by financial aid, are in a great position to conduct a long-term mission on behalf of their faith. Instead of thinking of themselves as a remnant of a defeated army they should regard themselves as a determined body of people ready to go forward in the work which is essentially dear to each one of them. The present is not a time for looking backward but for seizing the immense opportunities presented by the future.

Unitarian decline, however, has continued during the post-war period, just as it has for British institutional religion in general; in Britain and in Western Europe as a whole, church attendance is miniscule compared with that in North America. Moreover, religious education is included in the curriculum of British schools; thus one of the main factors motivating American families to attend church is absent. Some have suggested that the Assembly's organizational structure has handicapped efforts at renewal—that the emergence of leadership has been discouraged by both the large size of the governing council and the limited authority of the general secretary. Others have argued that a long-standing humanist-theist controversy has prevented the development of any clear identity and sense of mission.

Recently, the General Assembly was denied, first associate membership, then observer status, in the newly formed Council of Churches in Britain and Ireland. The Council is the successor to, and presumably more inclusive than, the British Council of Churches, of which the Assembly was an associate member. These rejections appear to reflect a growing feeling on the part of the orthodox Christian denominations that Unitarianism, with its increasing pluralism, has moved outside the Christian sphere and hence might better be engaged in interfaith rather than interchurch dialogue.

British Unitarians have long been internationally minded and have continued to maintain close ties with Unitarians in Canada, Australia, New Zealand, India, and South Africa, countries that are part of the British Commonwealth. The Australian and New Zealand Unitarian Association is affiliated with the General Assembly, as is the Canadian Unitarian Council; Margaret Barr and other Britons have supported the Unitarian movement in the Khasi Hills of India begun in the last century; the Free Protestant (Unitarian) Church of South Africa maintains fraternal relationship with the British Assembly. In addition, British Unitarians have provided significant support to the Unitarian churches in Romania and Hungary, both in the 1920s and the 1990s. The General Assembly has maintained close relations with the American Unitarian Association and its successor, the UUA, through ministerial exchanges (typically for six-month periods), visits to each other's annual meetings, and regular communication of information and ideas. The General Assembly and its predecessor, the British and Foreign Unitarian Association, have been active members of the IARF since its beginning, and the General Assembly is also actively involved in the International Council of Unitarians and Universalists, formed in 1995 on the initiative of David Usher, a British minister serving in the United States, and composed of more than a dozen national bodies.

As of 1995 there were 176 congregations in Great Britain (149 of them in England, 23 in Wales, some of them Welsh-speaking, and 4 in Scotland), plus 15 fellowships or groups (13 in England, and one each in Wales and on the Isle of Man). There were also 34 congregations in the Non-Subscribing Presbyterian Church of Ireland, mostly in the North. There were 144 ministers, 84 of them settled in churches or in paid denominational positions. The total membership for England, Wales, and Scotland was reported in 1996 as "roughly 8,000."

Publications include the *Inquirer*, published fortnightly; the *Unitarian*, monthly; *Faith and Freedom*, twice a year; and the *Transactions of the Unitarian Historical Society*, annually. Ministerial training takes place at Harris Manchester College, Oxford; Unitarian College Manchester; and Memorial College, Aberystwyth; the latter for Welsh-speaking candidates. In 1995 there were three ministerial students enrolled at Harris Manchester College, Oxford, and four at Unitarian College Manchester; the latter has close ties with the Unitarians in Romania and Hungary, and a number of ministers from those countries have studied there.

Recently signs of renewal in British Unitarianism have appeared, born of a realization in the last decade that positive measures needed to be taken if the movement was to survive and grow. A number of commissions were appointed to address the matters of objectives, extension, and education, including ministerial training. Out of the Objects Review Commission came a statement, presented to the General Assembly in 1990, identifying the following objectives:

To encourage and unite in membership those who uphold religious liberty unconstrained by the imposition of creeds;

To promote a free and inquiring religion through the worship of God and the celebration of life, the service of humanity and respect for all creation;

To uphold the liberal Christian position;

To affirm the liberal religious heritage and to learn from the spiritual, cultural and intellectual insights of all humanity;

To recognize the worth and dignity of all people and their freedom to believe as their consciences dictate.

The statement, based on the widest consultation of British Unitarian opinion ever made, was adopted by the General Assembly and ratified by a majority of the congregations that voted, but it failed to receive the high level of endorsement (90 percent) required to make it official. It stands, however, as broadly descriptive of contemporary British Unitarianism and indicates strong support for an inclusive, pluralistic understanding of the movement. It appears that the division between those who see Unitarianism as firmly rooted in Christianity and those who feel that it should represent a radical, liberal religious alternative may be at last on the wane.

Recently denominational leaders have reported a fresh spirit of optimism and hope. New worship materials—a book of special services and three hymnals—have recently been published, with the amount of recent hymn writing exceptionally high; in fact, the largest single contributor to the UUA hymnal, *Singing the Living Tradition*, was the British minister John Storey. Innovative rites of passage have been developed and attracted public attention. Recently an ambitious project for renewal has been undertaken called "Vision 2001," to be supported through a £1 million Millenium Fund. "The call," reported Peter Godfrey, a prominent minister, author, and editor, "is for us to be positive. To resist the temptation merely to hang on, hoping that 'something will turn up.' To be aware that merely struggling to survive is not enough. That survival depends upon vision and action to achieve the vision—making 'the seer's dream' into 'earthly fact.' At the centre, at the heart, is the *vision statement*: 'Our Unitarian Vision is to provide free and inquiring religion through the worship of God, the celebration of life, the service of humanity and respect for all creation. Unitarians will be a leading voice and example of liberal faith in Britain; providing welcoming and growing centres of inspiring worship and inclusive community; enriched by world faith traditions; committing ourselves to prophetic witness and social justice.'"

"That statement," stated Godfrey, "springs from faith—a faith aware of its roots, confident in its witness to the 'deep things of the spirit' and to freedom, reason and tolerance. This is the faith of the people of a religious movement in Great Britain who feel and believe that they are linked by a shared, common spirit and principles, and who wish to share their faith's joy and meaningfulness with as many people as possible."

Unitarianism in Europe has not been confined to Romania, Hungary, and Great Britain during the twentieth century. As of 1996, Unitarian organizations exist in at least twelve additional countries, with the number expected to grow.

Following the First World War, largely through the efforts of Charlotte Garrigue Masaryk, wife of the president of the Czechoslovakian Republic, a Unitarian church was established in Prague in 1921. Under the leadership of its minister, Norbert Capek, and his wife Maja, it grew into the largest Unitarian congregation in the world with a membership in 1932 of 3,395. It was there that the flower communion service, which has become widely used by American Unitarian Universalists, was developed. In 1941, Norbert Capek was arrested by the Nazis on charges of treason; a year later he was executed at the Dachau concentration camp in Germany. After the war, Unitarianism reemerged; there are presently congregations in Prague, Brno, Pilsen, and Litvinov, with a total membership of approximately 600, joined together in the Czech Unitarian Association under the leadership of Miloslav Starosta. Unfortunately, a long and bitter legal struggle has taken place over control of the Prague facilities and financial resources.

In Germany and the Netherlands there are a number of liberal religious organizations affiliated with the IARF, several bearing the Unitarian name, among them the Deutscher Unitarier-Bund and the Deutsche Unitarier Religiongemeinschaft.

The Association Unitarienne Francophone was organized in 1987 to bring together French-speaking Unitarians in France, Switzerland, and Belgium. It consists of three small groups in France at Paris, Nancy, and Digne and one in Geneva, Switzerland, plus scattered individual members.

There is one small Unitarian church in Denmark, founded in Copenhagen in 1900 and functioning as a lay-led fellowship.

A Unitarian fellowship was organized in Malmo, Sweden, in 1976. Eleven years later the first Swedish Unitarian minister, Ragnar Emilsen, was ordained, and the fellowship adopted the name Fria Kyrkan i Sverige (Free Church of Sweden).

A Unitarian Universalist congregation was founded in Riga, Latvia, in 1993 under the leadership of Vija Vetra.

The New Age Universalist Movement was started in Spain in 1992 as an intercultural, pluralistic organization by Jaume de Marcos, a Unitarian.

In 1994, Paul and Susan Sawyer, American Unitarian Universalist emissaries, together with their young son Alexander, helped to organize fellowships in Moscow and St. Petersburg, Russia, and Kiev, Ukraine. Subsequently another fellowship has been formed in Alushtya, Crimea, Ukraine. There had been no Unitarian congregations in Russia since the mid-seventeenth century.

Similarly, there had been no Unitarian congregations in Poland since 1660, when the Socinians were banished from the country. In the 1930s, Unitarianism was revived through the efforts of the Reverend Karol Grycz Smilowski, only to die out slowly, but in the 1980s it emerged again in the form of the Unitarian Universalist Community in Poland. The UUCP has congregations in Myslowice, Chorzow, Katowice, and Tarnowskie Gory. It would be heartwarming if Unitarianism could experience growth in Poland, one of the lands out of which it emerged.

European Unitarian Universalists is an organization of quite a different sort, being made up predominantly of American expatriates. Organized in 1981 as a European outpost of the UUA, it holds two retreats each year and publishes the *Unifier*, a quarterly newsletter. As of 1996 there were active fellowships, patterned closely after those in America, in Brussels, Belgium; the Netherlands; Paris, France; and Kaiserslautern, Wiesbaden, Heidelberg, and Augsburg-Munich, Germany.

As the twentieth century nears its end, it is evident that, in addition to the established movements in Romania, Hungary, and Great Britain, small but active centers of Unitarianism are continuing to spring up throughout Europe, and that an ever-growing network of relationships between them is in the process of formation. One can only wonder, what will the new century bring forth?

Conclusion

*A*ny study of Unitarianism makes abundantly clear that its expression is heavily influenced by the particular historical and cultural setting out of which it emerges and within which it exists. Thus any theological or statistical comparisons between Transylvanian and British Unitarianism, or between either of these and that in North America, are fraught with difficulties.

The setting in Poland, for example, made survival impossible; that in Transylvania has made theological change extraordinarily difficult; that in Britain has contributed to a decline in attendance and membership. In Britain, as in America, one becomes a member by choice, while in Transylvania one is typically born into Unitarianism, much as a child of Jewish parents is born into Judaism.

Within America, historical and cultural differences have led to marked, if not as dramatic, differences as well; for example, a New England congregation with roots going back to the seventeenth century is likely to express its Unitarianism quite differently than a California fellowship organized in the 1950s. Nevertheless, these differences are much less pronounced than those among the various European expressions or between any of the latter and those in America. As the twentieth century nears its end, historical and cultural differences continue to play an important part.

Earl Morse Wilbur proposed in the first volume of his history that, despite such differences, Unitarianism could be characterized by a growing commitment to three basic principles: freedom of religious thought, the unrestricted use of reason, and tolerance of differing views and practices. Some sixty years later, Wilbur's thesis still appears to be valid. This is not to imply that these three principles are confined to Unitarianism or that all individual Unitarians evidence commitment to them. Taken together, however, the three constitute a unique combination to which those groups identifying themselves as Unitarian have maintained an ongoing allegiance, regardless of geographical location.

It is not surprising that European Unitarians, as oppressed minorities whether in Poland, Transylvania, or the British Isles, should have made this commitment to freedom and tolerance; moreover, this commitment has continued once that oppression has ceased, as it has since 1813 in England and sporadically and briefly in Transylvania. The Diet of Torda in 1568 still stands firmly as the great landmark to this commitment. While this commitment originally was motivated by a corporate desire to be free from external oppression, it gradually has been internalized over the years to provide increasing individual freedom and tolerance within the Unitarian movement itself.

Through most of its history, the Unitarian commitment to reason focused on a rational interpretation of scripture. Then, as confidence in scripture as the sole source of religious understanding waned, reason began to be applied to other sources as well. Andrew Wiszowaty's *Rational Religion*, written in the late seventeenth century, stands out as an example of this change. Later, especially since the latter half of the nineteenth century, the use of reason increasingly has been supplemented by that of intuition and spirituality. Thus, James Martineau changed the course of British Unitarianism, and American Transcendentalists like Theodore Parker and Ralph Waldo Emerson have left their mark on Unitarianism in Transylvania. But while the use of reason has been modified, the basic principle remains firmly in place. Back at the beginning of the "Radical Reformation," the rational pioneers of the Unitarian movement and the Spirit-filled Anabaptists, many of whom were antitrinitarians and universalists, held much in common. The two movements soon went their separate ways, but perhaps the two traditions are again coming together.

It is possible that the twenty-first century may see the emergence of a commitment to pluralism as a *fourth* defining Unitarian principle, one emerging out of the internalized commitments to freedom and tolerance. Certainly the makeup of the International Council of Unitarians and Universalists suggests this, as does the roster of Unitarian groups presently existing in Europe. While tradition and the cultural climate in Romania may keep the Transylvanian Unitarians united in theology and practice, it is evident from the 1990 statement of the Objects Review Commission of the General Assembly that British Unitarianism is moving toward a pluralistic self-image not unlike that which American Unitarian Universalists have recently embraced. The most important question facing Unitarians in the next century may well be whether a pluralistic religious movement can survive and prosper.

Freedom, reason, tolerance, and pluralism are not, of course, adequate components of a religious faith in and of themselves—they can only provide the context in which faith can emerge, evolve, and live. Within its pluralism, Unitarianism will doubtless continue to take many theological and philosophical forms during the next century. However, a broad consensus may well be evolving around a principle expressed in the UUA covenant as "respect for the interdependent web of all existence of which we are a part." Significantly, at least one Transylvanian minister has asserted that this principle well embodies his own theology. Perhaps the traditional affirmation of *Egy az Isten*—God is One!—will point beyond itself and, while the nature of the Creator may remain a mystery, the Oneness of the Creation may become increasingly manifest.

References

Most of the topics covered in this book are based at least in part on material found in Earl Morse Wilbur's two-volume A History of Unitarianism, *the first volume of which, subtitled* Socinianism and Its Antecedents, *was published at Cambridge, Massachusetts, by the Harvard University Press in 1945; it will henceforth be referred to as Wilbur, Vol. 1. The second volume, subtitled* In Transylvania, England, and America, *was published by the same press in 1952; it will be referred to as Wilbur, Vol. 2. A significant number of references are to the third edition of George Huntston Williams's* The Radical Reformation, *published by Sixteenth Century Journal Publishers, Inc., Kirkville, Missouri, in 1992; it will be referred to simply as Williams.*

"As for the Trinity..."
Major Sources: Wilbur, Vol. I, Chapters I-IV. Williams, Chapters 6, 7, 13, and 14.

Other Sources: Roland H. Bainton, *Hunted Heretic: The Life and Death of Michael Servetus* (Boston: Beacon Press, 1953), pp. 6-7, 10-11, 21-31, 34-35. Bainton, *The Reformation of the Sixteenth Century* (Boston: Beacon Press, 1952), pp. 77-94, 144-52. Tim Dowley, organizing editor, *Eerdmans' Handbook to the History of Christianity* (Herts, England: Lion Publishing, 1977), pp. 109-13, 134-35, 156-60, 230-31, 314-23, 348, 352-53, 360-81. Elaine Pagels, *The Gnostic Gospels* (New York: Vintage Books, 1981), pp. 70-72. Hosea Ballou II, *Ancient History of Universalism* (Boston: Universalist Publishing House, 1885), pp. 266-81. Owen Chadwick, *The Reformation* (London: Penguin Books, 1964), Chapters 1-3, 6. Mitchell B. Garrett, *European History, 1500-1815* (New York: American Book Company, 1940), Chapters 8-10.

Source of Opening Quotation: David B. Parke, *The Epic of Unitarianism* (Boston: Beacon Press, 1957), p. 1.

Sources of Other Quotations: Bainton, *Hunted Heretic*, pp. 67-68, for first quote from Melanchthon; Wilbur, Vol. I, p. 70, for second. Wilbur, Vol. I, p. 4, for quote from Wilbur. *Eerdmans' Handbook*, p. 158, for quote from creed adopted at Council of Nicaea. Harry Emerson Fosdick, editor, *Great Voices of the Reformation* (New York: Random House, 1952), p. 156, for quote from Zwingli. *Eerdmans' Handbook*, p. 380, for quote from Calvin. Williams, p. 302, for hymn by Haetzer.

The Life and Death of Michael Servetus

Major Sources: Wilbur, Vol. I, Chapters V, IX-XII. Williams, Chapters 1, 8, 10 (Part II), 11, 23. Bainton, *Hunted Heretic*, Chapters 1-11.

Other Sources: Bainton, *The Travail of Religious Liberty* (New York: Harper Torchbooks, 1951), Chapters 2, 3. Chadwick, *The Reformation*, pp. 197-99. Garrett, pp. 151-52.

Source of Opening Quotation: Bainton, *Hunted Heretic*, p. 62.

Sources of Other Quotations: Bainton, *Hunted Heretic*, pp. 18-20, 47, 51, 74, 142, 197, 200, 200-01, 212; Williams, pp. 56, 308, 403; and Wilbur, pp. 53, 55, for quotes from Servetus. Bainton, *Hunted Heretic*, pp. 144-45, 209, 210; and Wilbur, Vol. I, pp. 168-69, for quotes from Calvin. Bainton, *Hunted Heretic*, p. 10, for quote from Luther. Bainton, *Hunted Heretic*, p. 52, for quote from Oecolampadius. Bainton, *Hunted Heretic*, p. 71, for quote from Inquisition. Wilbur, Vol. I, p.144, for quote from Wilbur. Bainton, *Hunted Heretic*, pp. 152-53, 156, for quotes from Trie. Bainton, *Hunted Heretic*, p. 168, for quote from Genevan Consistory. Bainton, *Hunted Heretic*, p. 209, for quote from Geneva Council.

The Double Legacy of Michael Servetus
Major Sources: Wilbur, Vol. I, Chapters VI, VII, VIII, XIII-XVII. Williams, Chapters 23, 24; pp. 1048, 1154-55, 1230.

Other Sources: Bainton, *The Travail of Religious Liberty*, Chapter 4. Wilbur, Vol. II, pp. 29, 35, 41-42, 148. Stefan Zweig, *The Right to Heresy: Castellio Against Calvin* (Boston: Beacon Press, 1951), pp. 156, 159, 172-73. John C. Godbey, Distinguished Scholar's Address, Collegium Conference, Craigville, Massachusetts, October 13, 1995.

Source of Opening Quotation: Bainton, *The Travail of Religious Liberty*, pp. 107, 120.

Sources of Other Quotations: Wilbur, Vol. I, p. 191, for quote from Wilbur. Zweig, pp. 156, 159; Williams, p. 961, for quotes from "Martin Bellius". Wilbur, Vol. I, pp. 198, 199, for quotes from Beza. Zweig, pp. 172-73; Wilbur, Vol. I, p. 203, for quote from Castellio. Wilbur, Vol. I, p. 210, for quote from Wilbur. Wilbur, Vol. I, p. 79, for quote from Melanchthon. Wilbur, Vol. I, p. 85, for Anabaptists' ten points of doctrine. Williams, p. 1154, for quote from Ochino. Williams, p. 966, for quotes from Laelius Socinus. Wilbur, Vol. I, p. 227, for quote from Alciati. Wilbur, Vol. I, p. 225, for quote from Calvin.

Faustus Socinus and the Rise of Polish Socinianism
Major Source: Wilbur, Vol. I, Chapters XXIII-XXXII.

Other Sources: Wilbur, Vol. I, Chapters XIX-XXII. Williams, Chapters 24, 25, 29. Stanislas Kot, *Socinianism in Poland*, translated by Earl Morse Wilbur (Boston: Starr King Press, 1957), Introduction and Chapter 9. Godbey, address, Collegium Conference, 1995. Bainton, *Women of the Reformation* (Minneapolis, MN: Augsburg Publishing House, 1977), p. 160.

Source of Opening Quotation: Parke, pp. 25-26.

Sources of Other Quotations: Kot, pp. xi-xii, for quote from synod at Secemin. Wilbur, Vol. I, pp. 334-35, for quote from chronicler of 1565 meeting, Minor Church. Wilbur, Vol. I, p. 347, for quote from statement of 1567 synod. Kot, p. 50, for quote from Polish Calvinists on Raków. Wilbur, Vol. I, p. 361, for quote from British visitor to Raków. Wilbur, Vol. I, pp. 363-64, for quote from Confederation of Warsaw. Wilbur, Vol. I, p. 395, for quote from Wilbur. Wilbur, Vol. I, p. 403, for quote from Faustus Socinus.

The Persecution and Destruction of the Socinian Church

Major Source: Wilbur, Vol. I, Chapters XXXIV-XXXIX, XLIV.

Other Sources: Wilbur, Vol. I, Chapters XL-XLIII. George Huntston Williams, editor, *The Polish Brethren*, Part 2, Harvard Theological Studies XXX (Missoula, Montana: Scholars Press, 1980), pp. 591-623, 636-39, 685-701.

Source of Opening Quotation: Williams, editor, *The Polish Brethren*, p. 639.

Sources of Other Quotations: Wilbur, Vol. I, p. 455, for quote from Socinian lamenter over Raków. Williams, *The Polish Brethren*, pp. 661-63, for quotes from Przypkowski. Wilbur, Vol. I, p. 482, for quote from Wiszowaty's opponent. Wilbur, Vol. I, pp. 583-84, for quote from Preface, *Racovian Catechism*. Williams, *The Polish Brethren*, p. 686, for quote from *Racovian Catechism* concerning resurrection. Wilbur, Vol. I, p. 521, for quote from Wilbur.

Francis Dávid and the Rise of Unitarianism in Transylvania

Major Sources: Wilbur, Vol. II, Chapters I-V, Chapter VI, pp. 81-83. Williams, Chapter 28. John Erdö, *Transylvanian Unitarian Church: Chronological History and Theological Essays*, translated by Judit Gellérd (Chico, California: Center for Free Religion, 1990), pp. 5-15.

Other Sources: Gellérd Imre, "Truth Liberates You", translated by Gellérd Judit (Chico, CA: Center for Free Religion, 1990); Wilbur, Vol. I, p. 484; Kot, p. xix.

Source of Opening Quotation: Erdö, p. 7.
Sources of Other Quotations: Erdo, pp. 7-8, for quote from chronicler. Parke, pp. 19-20, for quote from Act of Religious Toleration and Freedom of Conscience. Wilbur, Vol. II, p. 37, for quote from orthodox historian concerning disputation. Wilbur, Vol. II, p. 40, for quotes from King John Sigismund. Wilbur, Vol. II, p. 43, for quote from Dávid's opponent following Várad debate. Wilbur, Vol. II, p. 61, for quote from diet's decree of 1576. Wilbur, Vol. II, pp. 68-69, for quote from resolution of Torda synod of 1578. Wilbur, Vol. I, p. 71, for David's four theses. Wilbur, Vol. II, p. 73, for quote from conclusion of Dávid's last sermon. Gellérd, pp. 10-11, for quote from Dávid's last sermon. Gellérd, p. 45, for quote from Dávid concerning the Holy Spirit. Erdö, p. 15, for Dávid's inscription on dungeon cell wall.

Transylvanian Unitarianism: Its Persistence Through Travail

Major Sources: Wilbur, Vol. II, Chapters VI-IX. Erdö, pp. 14-33.

Other Source: Joseph Ferencz, *Hungarian Unitarianism in the Nineteenth and Twentieth Centuries* (Chico, California: Center for Free Religion, 1990), Chapters I-IV.

Source of Opening Quotations: Judit Gellérd, Introduction, *In Storm, Even Trees Lean on Each Other* (Chico, California: Center for Free Religion, 1993), p. 10.

Sources of Other Quotations: Wilbur, Vol. II, p. 96, for quote from Dávid concerning Jesuits. Wilbur, Vol. II, p. 105, for quote from Jesuit claim of Unitarians forsaking gospel. Wilbur, Vol. II, p. 119, for quote from Unitarian leader concerning Dées agreement. Wilbur, Vol. II, p. 126, for quote from 1686 accord with Leopold I concerning religious freedom. Wilbur, Vol. II, p. 130, for quote from Wilbur concerning Kolozsvár fire. Erdö, p. 22, for quote from Prince Joseph. Erdö, p. 32, for quote from Berde.

The Beginnings of Unitarianism in England
Major Source: Wilbur, Vol. II, Chapters X-XV.
   Other Sources: Williams, Chapters 14, 30. Parke, pp. 29-
47. Alexander Gordon, *Heads of Unitarian History* (Portway,
Bath, England: Cedric Chivers, Ltd., 1970), pp. 3-44. Garrett,
Chapters XI, XIX, XXIV. Jeremy Goring, "Unitarianism: His-
tory, Myth, or Make-believe?" *Transactions of the Unitarian
Historical Society*, Vol. XIX, No. 4 (April 1990): pp. 213-27.
   Source of Opening Quotation: Gordon, p. 3.
   Sources of Other Quotations: Wilbur, Vol. II, p. 271, for
quote from Anglican subscription. Wilbur, Vol. II, p. 273, for
quote from minister concerning Athanasian Creed. Wilbur,
Vol. II, p. 279, for quote from petition to Parliament. Wilbur,
Vol. II, p. 168, for quote from Wilbur. Williams, p. 1197, for
quote from van Parris. Williams, p. 1196, for quote from
Assheton. Wilbur, Vol. II, p. 172, for quote from Philpot.
Williams, p. 1202, for quote from bishop returning from
exile. Williams, p. 1206, for quote concerning the five "with a
fagot tied on their shoulders." Wilbur, Vol. II, p. 179, for quote
from historian concerning king's punishment of heretics.
Eerdmans' Handbook, p. 388, for quote from James I. Wilbur,
Vol. II, p. 192, for quote from Draconic Ordinance. Goring, p.
218, for quote from British historian. Wilbur, Vol. II, p. 213,
for quote from member of Parliament concerning Socinian
books. Wilbur, Vol. II, p. 245, for quote from Emlyn's
jury. Wilbur, Vol. II, p. 246, for quote from the bishop sympathetic to Emlyn. Wilbur, Vol. II, p. 263, for quote from church
leader concerning Salters' Hall conference. Wilbur, Vol. II,
pp. 269-70, for quote concerning nonsubscribing churches.

British Unitarianism: Its Emergence and Maturation
as a Movement
Major Source: Wilbur, Vol. II, pp. 286-92; Chapters XVI-XIX;
pp. 395-98.

Other Sources: Gordon, pp. 52-53, 102-26. Peter Godfrey, "What Is, and What Has Unitarianism Been in Great Britain," *Remembering Our Past, Trusting Our Future*, Sesquicentennial Commemorative Booklet, Meadville/Lombard Theological School, 1995, pp. 3-12. Parke, pp. 68-72, 75-76. V. D. Davis, *A History of Manchester College* (London: George Allen & Unwin, Ltd., 1932), pp. 147-48, 168-69. Clinton Lee Scott, *These Live Tomorrow* (Boston: Beacon Press, 1964), pp. 21-31. John Ruskin Clark, *Joseph Priestley: A Comet in the System* (San Diego: Torch Publications, 1990), pp. 114-15, 234. Charles A. Howe, "British Universalism, 1787-1825: Elhanan Winchester, William Vidler, and the Gospel of Universal Restoration," *Transactions of the Unitarian Historical Society*, Vol. XVII, No. 1 (September 1979): pp. 1-14. Letter, David L. Wykes to Howe, 4 June 1996.

Source of Opening Quotation: Davis, p. 15.

Source of Other Quotations: Wilbur, Vol. II, p. 292, for quote from Lindsey. Gordon, pp. 123-24, 124, for quotes from Gordon on Mary Priestley. Gordon, p. 125, for quote from Mary Priestley. Clark, p. 234, for quote from Channing. Wilbur, Vol. II, p. 360, for quote from Wilbur on Lady Hewley decision. Wilbur, Vol. II, p. 367, for quote from Wellbeloved. R. K. Webb, *Truth, Liberty, Religion: Essays Celebrating Two Hundred Years of Manchester College*, 1996, for quote from Letter, Martineau to R. L. Carpenter, 25 April 1885.

The Twentieth Century: A Brief Overview
Major Sources: Wilbur, Vol. II, pp. 157-65, 375. Erdö, pp. 33-41. Ferencz, pp. 32-49. Interview with Bishop János Erdö, Kolozsvár, 24 April 1996. Godfrey, pp. 3-5, 11-12.

Other Sources: Gellérd Imre, *A Burning Kiss from God: Four Centuries of Transylvanian Unitarian Preaching*, translated by Gellérd Judit, preface by George M. Williams (Chico, California: Center for Free Religion, 1990). Emerson Hugh Lalone, *And Thy Neighbor as Thyself: A Story of Universalist Social*

Action (Boston: Universalist Publishing House, 1959), pp. 105-7. Conversations with the Reverends Dénes Katona, Székelyderzs, 21 April 1996; Mózes Kedei, Székelyudvarhely, 23 April 1996; and B. Ferenc Bálint, Kolozsvár, 24 April 1996. Letters from Judit Gellérd, 3 July 1996; Donald S. Harrington, 29 May 1996; and Richard Beal, 30 May 1996. UU *World*, May/June 1990, July/August 1991, July/August 1995. "A Brief History of the Orbán Balázs Gymnasium of Székelykeresztúr," Bicentennial Memorial, 1994, pp. 91-2. Peter Raible, *First Days Record*, March 1996, pp. 38-9. "Partner Church News," Newsletter of the Partner Church Council, April 1996, p. 20. Goring, p. 217. Parke, p. 76. Mary Lawrance, *"Khublei": The Story of the Khasi Hills Liberal Churches* (California: Friends of Margaret Barr, 1964). Letters from Alan Ruston, June 1996, 21 August 1996; Matthew Smith, 30 May 1996; Phillip Hewett, 25 June 1996; Andrew Hill, June 1996; and David Usher, 10 June 1996. UUA Directory, 1995-96, pp. 374-83. UUA Directory, 1996-97, pp. 420-26. "The Global Chalice," Newsletter of the International Council of Unitarians and Universalists, July 1996. David B. Parke in *A Stream of Light*, Conrad Wright, editor (Boston: UUA, 1975), p. 105. Orloff Miller, Renate Bauer, and Glenn Erasmus Bauer, "Feathers of the Firebird," Ludwigshafen, Germany, 1995.

Source of Opening Quotation: UUA Directory, 1994, p. 372.

Source of Other Quotations: Erdö, p. 34, for inscription on plaque at Déva. George M. Williams, Preface in Gellérd, *A Burning Kiss from God*, p. 4, for quote from Gellérd. Parke, *The Epic of Unitarianism*, p. 76, for quote from "The Work of the Churches". Letter from Hill, for quote from Objects Review Commission. Godfrey, pp. 11-12, for quote from Godfrey. Godfrey, pp. 11-12, for quote from Vision Statement.

Selected Bibliography

Bainton, Roland H. *Hunted Heretic: The Life and Death of Michael Servetus.* Boston: Beacon Press, 1953.

_____. *The Reformation of the Sixteenth Century.* Boston: Beacon Press, 1952.

Erdö, John. *Transylvanian Unitarian Church: Chronological History and Theological Essays.* Translated by Judit Gellérd. Chico, California: Center for Free Religion, 1990.

Gellérd, Imre. *"Truth Liberates You": The Message of Transylvania's First Unitarian Bishop.* Translated by Gellérd Judit. Chico, California: Center for Free Religion, 1990.

Gordon, Alexander. *Heads of Unitarian History.* Portway, Bath, England: Cedric Chivers, Ltd., 1970.

Goring, Jeremy. "Unitarianism: History, Myth or Make-believe?" *Transactions of the Unitarian Historical Society,* Vol. XIX, No. 4 (April 1990): pp. 213-27.

Kot, Stanislav. *Socinianism in Poland.* Translated by Earl Morse Wilbur. Boston: Starr King Press, 1957.

Wilbur, Earl Morse. *A History of Unitarianism: Socinianism and Its Antecedents.* Cambridge, Massachusetts: Harvard University Press, 1945.

_____. *A History of Unitarianism: In Transylvania, England, and America.* Cambridge, Massachusetts: Harvard University Press, 1952.

Williams, George Huntston. *The Radical Reformation.* 3rd ed. Kirkville, Missouri: Sixteenth Century Journal Publishers, Inc., 1992.

_____, ed. *The Polish Brethren.* Part 2. Harvard Theological Studies XXX. Missoula, Montana: Scholars Press, 1980.

Chronology

325	Council of Nicaea affirms deity of Christ
c. 475	Athanasian Creed makes doctrine of the Trinity specific
1517	Martin Luther posts ninety-five theses in Wittenberg, Germany; Protestant Reformation begins
1531	Michael Servetus publishes *On the Errors of the Trinity*
1553	Servetus publishes *The Restoration of Christianity*
1553	Servetus tried in Geneva, Switzerland, and executed; age about forty-three
1554	Sebastian Castellio publishes *Concerning Heretics*
1565	Synod at Brzeziny marks start of Minor Reformed Church in Poland
1568	Diet of Torda, Act of Religious Toleration; Unitarianism begins in Transylvania under Francis Dávid's leadership
1569	Raków established as Socinian center in Poland
1571	Unitarianism recognized in Transylvania as an official "received religion"; King John Sigismund dies
1572	Law against religious innovation enacted in Transylvania
1579	Trial, imprisonment, and death of Dávid
1579	Faustus Socinus arrives in Poland
1604	Faustus Socinus dies at age sixty-four
1605	*Racovian Catechism* first published at Raków
1637	Accord of Deés further restricts Unitarian freedom in Transylvania
1639	Raków destroyed by Roman Catholics
1655	John Biddle banished from England for Unitarian views
1658	Decree of banishment forces Socinians from Poland
1662	"Great Ejection" follows passage of Act of Uniformity by Parliament in England
1665	Five Mile Act by Parliament restricts Dissenters' activities

1689   Act of Toleration by Parliament gives Dissenters more freedom

1716   Roman Catholics retake the Great Church in Kolozsvár, Transylvania

1719   Salters' Hall conference in London divides Dissenters

1774   Theophilus and Hannah Lindsey establish Essex Street Chapel, first Unitarian congregation in England

1791   Riots in Birmingham, England; Joseph Priestley's Unitarian church and home attacked because of his liberal views

1794   Priestleys move to America

1813   Trinity Act; denial of doctrine no longer a crime in England

1825   British and Foreign Unitarian Association established

1844   Dissenters' Chapel Act gives English Unitarians title to their places of worship

1858   Relations established between British and Transylvanian Unitarians

1882   National Conference of Unitarian . . . and Other Non-Subscribing or Kindred Congregations formed in Great Britain

1900   International Association for Religious Freedom established

1921   Treaty of Trianon; Transylvania ceded to Romania by Hungary

1921   Unitarian Church established in Prague under Norbert Capek, soon becomes largest Unitarian church in world

1928   General Assembly of Unitarian and Free Christian Churches formed in Great Britain through merger of National Conference and British and Foreign Unitarian Association

1942   Capek executed by the Nazis

1946   Oppression of Transylvanian Unitarians by Communists begins

1989   Ceausescu dictatorship overthrown in Romania; Part-

ner Church Project with North American congregations begins
1995   International Council of Unitarians and Universalists
formed

Pronunciation Table

The text contains many names that the reader, unaided, might find difficult to pronounce. Names from the more common languages of western Europe are presumed to offer no particular difficulty, but Polish and Hungarian follow different rules. The table here given is designed to help the reader by indicating approximately correct pronunciations.

In Polish the accent is invariably on the penult; in Hungarian, on the first syllable. The marks over vowels in Hungarian denote not accent but a long vowel sound.

In the table below,

> N denotes the nasal *n* as in French words
> ñ is to be pronounced *ny* as in the American Spanish *cañon*
> *zh* is like *z* in *azure*, or the French *j*
> *e* is given the short sound
> *ö* and *ü* are sounded as in German
> LY sounds as in *halyard*

Agh (awg)
Almási (awl´-mah-she)
Augusztinovics (ow´-goos-tin-o-vich)
Báthory (bah´-to-ry)
Beke (be´-ke)
Brzeziny (bzhezh eé-ny)
Boldizsar (bol´-dizh-ahr)
Cluj (cloozh)
Dajka (doy´-kaw)
Dávid (dah´-vid)
Deés (de´-aysh)
Déva (day´-vaw)
Enyedi (en´-yed-ee)

Ferencz (fer´-ents)
Gyulafehérvár (joo´-law-fe-hayr-vahr)
Hunyadi (hoon´-yaw-dee)
Imre (im´-re)
János (yahn´-osh)
Józef (yoo´-zhef)
Keserüi (kesh´-e-rü-ee)
Kolozsvár (kol´-ozh-vahr)
Koncz (konts)
Kossuth (kosh´-oot)
Kraków (krah´-koof)
Lázár (lah´-zahr)
Luclawice (loots-wah-veet´-see)
Magyar (mawd´-yawr)
Mélius (may´-lee-oosh)
Mózes (mo´-zesh)
Pál (pahl)
Przypkowski (pzhip-kof´-skee)
Raków (rah´-koof)
Ráv (rahv)
Sigismund (sij´-iss-mund)
Suki (shoo´-kee)
Székely (say´-keLY)
Szekler (sek-ler)
Szentábrahámi (sent-ahb´-raw-haw-mee)
Szent-Iványi (sent´ iv-ahn-ye)
Torda (tor´-daw)
Toroczkai (tor´-ots-koy)
Trauzner (trowts´-ner)
Tyszkiewicz (tys-kye´-vich)
Várad (vah´-rawd)
Wiszowaty (vish-o-vah´-ty)

Note: The material in this pronunciation table is taken from Wilbur, Vol. I, pp. 589-92, and Wilbur, Vol. II, pp. 488-91.

Index